Elegant but Easy Cookbook

ELEGANT
BUT EASY
COOKBOOK

Marian Fox Burros
and
Lois Levine

REVISED EDITION

Illustrated by Rosalie Petrash Schmidt

COLLIER BOOKS
Macmillan Publishing Company
New York

COLLIER MACMILLAN PUBLISHERS
London

Macmillan Publishing Company
866 Third Avenue, New York, N.Y. 10022
Collier Macmillan Canada, Inc.

Library of Congress Cataloging in Publication Data
Burros, Marian Fox.
  Elegant but easy cookbook.
  Includes index.
  1. Cookery.   2. Entertaining.   I. Levine, Lois.
II. Title.
TX740.B82   1984   641.5   84-9997
ISBN 0-02-009340-3

Macmillan books are available at special discounts for bulk
purchases for sales promotions, premiums, fund-raising,
or educational use. Special editions or book excerpts can
also be created to specification. For details, contact:
Special Sales Director
Macmillan Publishing Company
866 Third Avenue
New York, New York 10022

FIRST COLLIER BOOKS EDITION 1968

22   21   20   19   18

Portions of this book appeared previously in *Elegant But
Easy*, copyright © 1960 by Marian Fox Burros and Lois
Liebeskind Levine, and in *Second Helpings*, copyright
© 1963 by Marian F. Burros and Lois L. Levine.

Printed in the United States of America

Contents

Elegant but Easy Cookbook

Introduction

WRITING an introduction turns out to be a more difficult task than collecting, testing, and writing recipes. However, a word or two about this book may interest our readers, some of whom will remember certain parts from our previous book, titled *Elegant but Easy*.* We had our share of trials and tribulations before that book was accepted by our eventual publisher and issued in paperback form. But its acceptance by our readers has been so gratifying and continuous that we were asked to edit and expand the original version, and the result is what you are reading now. Although *Elegant but Easy* was the basis for this work, we went through it carefully, editing and deleting, but most especially adding, to make this volume as complete and useful as possible.

This new and expanded cookbook should prove as helpful

* Collier Books, 1961.

to new readers as the former has been. We dedicate it to all those who have written to tell us they have worn their original *Elegant but Easy* to shreds. (We hope *they* will replace it with this more permanent form.) The new recipes are as elegant to serve and easy to consume, thanks to advance preparation by the cook, as the old ones we have retained have proven to be. This, naturally, leads us to answer your question, "How?"

We believe entertaining really should be fun, for the hostess as well as the guests. The qualities of a pleasant party are often intangible, but good company and delicious food contribute a great deal to the guests' enjoyment. The hostess, too, should be able to participate and not have to spend her time in the kitchen cooking, tasting, and seasoning. So few of us have help today! This does not mean, however, that everything should come from the precooked or instant section of your grocers' shelves. You can prepare *Elegant but Easy* meals with no help and still enjoy the company of your guests. We'd like to show you how.

Of course there must be congenial guests, and choosing a convivial group is as important as choosing the right combination of foods. An almost scientific set of rules for selecting a guest list begins with the "do-nots":

DO NOT invite an entire clique or group of close friends at one time. Rather try to add a new couple to an established group or introduce couples you feel would enjoy each other's company. This way, even if the talk returns to gardening or babies, it will be new gardens and new babies.

DO NOT bunch "categories"—all your doctor friends at one time would be deadly though antiseptic—together unless you have a very specific purpose: a birthday, a shower, a family gathering, a meeting of the American Medical Association!

DO NOT try to wipe out all your obligations at one fell swoop. Guests catch on quickly to your motives and determine not to enjoy themselves!

So much for your guest list; every rule is here to be broken.

Whatever you enjoy, no doubt the rest of your company will, too. Just do not, please, have ten lawyers and one engineer!

The number of your guests, as well as the space you have available, influences your menu. For experimenting with something new invite the couple next door or your closest friends, informally. Note that many of these recipes are written for four servings. As a matter of fact, our neighbors —not to mention the authors—have grown plump helping us get together this book, as every recipe has been carefully tested and tasted! In a small apartment dinners for six or eight are probably all that can be handled comfortably for both cook and guests. If you have the room and wish to entertain twenty for dinner, a buffet—with two or three entrees—would be as effective as a formal sitdown dinner. Please, please, however, when serving a buffet, do not expect your guests to balance plates on their knees. Provide some kind of table; bridge tables are good, or those handy little stack tables that are so popular.

Whenever possible, it is fun to set a theme for your party; any happy occasion: a birthday, anniversary, new home, new job, new bride, new couple in town. Or let the menu set the theme such as a Chinese dinner, an Italian feast, a curry supper. Vary the usual party fare! Your flowers, table decor, and invitations (if you are so inclined) with your menu complete the picture.

The foods you serve need not be expensive to be *elegant* and the recipes need not be oversimplified to be *easy*. The ease comes at serving time thanks to advance preparation. Foods need not be prepared at the last minute to be impressive. Soups, though elegant, require extra dishes and often entail extra bother for the servantless hostess, who can avoid last-minute pot-watching by serving the first course in the form of hors d'oeuvres during the cocktail hour. Lobster soufflé is divine, but so is Chicken Imperial. Serve on your best platter, use your best table service and linens, and put your best foot forward. You can be confident of success thanks to careful planning. The meal is set well in advance, there are no details to be completed at the zero hour. You are a guest at your own party!

The "how-to" is the basis for this cookbook. We have incorporated many recipes for foods that can be prepared one or more days in advance and lose nothing in standing. Such recipes are designated by a "#" followed by a numeral, representing the number of days in advance such food may safely be prepared and refrigerated. Other recipes are marked with an "*" to denote that they are freezable. (For example: *#2 Chafing-Dish Meat Balls—these can either be prepared two days in advance and refrigerated, or considerably in advance and then frozen.) With the exception of a few ice-cream dishes, or unless otherwise noted, these frozen foods should be removed from the freezer the night before serving to allow ample time for thorough defrosting. We have also included some "quickies" for last minute guests.

As an example, let us prepare a formal menu and plan it to allow the hostess to be genuinely relaxed when the guests arrive.

Toasted Mushroom Rolls
Tuna-cheese Spread
Chicken Divan   Cornflaked Potatoes
Spinach Tart   Orange-coconut Mold
Heat-and-Serve Rolls
Chocolate Roll   Coffee

If the party is given on Saturday night, sometime before Thursday, even two or three weeks in advance, you should prepare the mushroom rolls, chicken and chocolate roll. Wrap and freeze.

Do your marketing Wednesday. Thursday make the mold, the potatoes. Friday make the spinach tart, and the tuna spread. Your refrigerator may bulge a bit, but it will be very, very empty on Sunday.

Saturday, the day of the party, set the table, defrost the chicken, chocolate roll and mushroom rolls. Then take a nap! An hour before the guests arrive, fix the pot for coffee. One-half hour before, set the mushroom rolls on a cookie sheet, ready to pop in the oven as soon as the first guests arrive. Reheat the chicken, brown the rolls and potatoes in the oven. You are really all set as the doorbell rings.

What about a luncheon Wednesday, for another example:

Melon-mint Cocktails
Piquant Crab Casserole   *Pineapple-lime Mold*
Savory Bread
Macaroon Pie   *Coffee*

And here's the way to schedule the cooking. Anytime in advance of Monday prepare the crab casserole and freeze. The week of your party, on Monday, prepare the melon cocktail and the pineapple mold. Tuesday prepare the bread and macaroon pie. Tuesday night defrost the casserole. Wednesday morning set the table. Whip a bowl of cream with which to top the pie and get your coffee maker set to go.

Forty minutes before you are ready to sit down, heat the crab casserole. Put the bread in the oven. And now await your guests.

This is all very well you say, but suppose guests arrive unexpectedly. How is it possible to relax and enjoy them, when you are frantically pulling together a meal? Well it isn't as easy as knowing two weeks in advance, but it can be done. Be prepared. Keep in your freezer or on your shelf a few already cooked or practically cooked meals. Then you can't be caught short!

Have a crab and mushroom casserole in your freezer. This dish needs only to be heated without defrosting to be served. Keep ingredients for shrimp Newburg, quick chow mein, or bachelor crabmeat handy and always have at least one dessert in the freezer: applesauce cake, brownies, ice cream. Have nuts, a jar of fudge sauce and coconut, etc., and you have the makings of a "Do-It-Yourself Sundae." Everyone will think you sent out to a local catering service!

Now let's tackle something on a large scale—carefully

thought out and prepared. For example a cocktail party on a Sunday afternoon.

Judiciously combine hot and cold hors d'oeuvres such as: biscuit hors d'oeuvres filled with bacon and tiny franks. These may be frozen and merely heated at party time. Also make and freeze cheese shorties and chafing-dish meatballs. Miniature pizzas may be put together and frozen, then defrosted and put under the broiler for a few minutes before serving.

In the dip department, try one bowl of red caviar dip and one of fruit of the sea. These may easily be prepared two days ahead.

For cold hors d'oeuvres—smoked salmon pinwheels which should be frozen and tiny cream puffs, some filled with ham and some with cream cheese and Roquefort. The puffs may be frozen and merely reheated the day of your party to rejuvenate them. Pâté as well as the cheese filling may be made a day in advance and used to fill the puffs the morning of the party. One more beautiful as well as delicious addition to your table might be *Pâté en Gelée* which can be made the day before. The menu provides adequate quantity and selection for forty guests. It will also give you a colorful and interesting table. It would be divine to have a woman in the kitchen heating the hors d'oeuvres, etc., but you, yourself, can put them in the oven and still be the smiling, cheerful hostess.

We have tried to make each recipe as clear and concise as possible, so that the book can be used by a bride as well as an experienced cook. We hope that you will enjoy using it, as we certainly have enjoyed putting it together.

Lois Levine and Marian Burros

Helpful Information in Buying

THERE may have been a good reason for numbering cans (2½, 303, etc.) in the dim, dark past. But the reason is pretty obscure today. Especially since a No. 2½ can may contain anywhere from 28 to 30 ounces. (We're all for standardizing can sizes after we spend four hours in the grocery store trying to pin down some of these elusive numbers.)

Throughout the book we designate the size can required by the number of ounces it contains. But don't take it so literally that you will bypass a 1-pound 12-ounce can if the recipe calls for a 1-pound 13-ounce can. Maybe your store doesn't carry that size.

And for those who would like a short but not too accurate course in what the numbers mean, see the following chart.

CAN SIZE	APPROXIMATE WEIGHT	CUPFULS
6 oz	6 oz	¾
8 oz	8 oz	1
No. 1	10 to 12 oz	1¼ to 1½
No. 300	14 oz to 1 lb	1¾
No. 1½ or 303	1 lb to 17 oz	2
No. 2	1 lb 4 oz or 1 pint 2 fl. oz	2½
No. 2½	1 lb. 12 oz to 1 lb 14 oz	3½
No. 3 cylinder or 46 oz	3 lbs 3 oz or 1 quart 14 oz	5¾
No. 10	6 lbs 2 oz to 7 lbs 5 oz	12 to 13

I : Elegant but Easy
Hors D'oeuvres

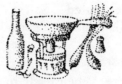

Hot Hors D'oeuvres

Artichokes Ramaki

#1 *about 2 dozen*

Cook according to package directions

1 package frozen artichoke hearts (9 oz or about 24)

Drain and sprinkle with

Onion salt

Cut crosswise in half about

12 slices bacon

Wrap each half-slice around each artichoke heart. Refrigerate. To serve, broil 6 inches from heat about 8 minutes, turning once.

Bacon and Cheese Canapés

*#2   3 dozen

Mix together well

2 tablespoons butter   ½ teaspon paprika
8 oz cheddar cheese, grated   Salt
8 slices bacon, cooked and   Pepper
  finely chopped   2 eggs
½ teaspoon dry mustard

Refrigerate or freeze. When ready to serve, spread on toast rounds and brown under broiler.

Biscuit Hors D'oeuvres

*#1   4 dozen

These have a catered look about them!

1 can refrigerator biscuits

Flatten each biscuit with palm of your hand. Cut each biscuit into quarters. In each quarter wrap

1 cocktail frankfurter with   sliver of cheese in slit

Refrigerate or freeze. To serve, bake at 450° F for about 5 minutes—until crisp.

Blintzes—Never Fail

*#2   *Old-fashioned recipe with exact proportions*

FILLING

Press

1 lb farmer cheese

through ricer or fine strainer

Mix with

1 egg   1 tablespoon soft butter
1 tablespoon sugar   Pinch salt

BATTER

Beat until light and foamy

2 eggs

Add

½ teaspoon salt	1 tablespoon melted butter
1 teaspoon sugar	1 cup flour, sifted with
1 cup water	¼ teaspoon baking powder

Beat until smooth. Drop this batter, 2 tablespoons at a time, onto greased (5-inch) frying pan, on medium heat. Tip pan so batter spreads thinly over entire pan. Pour off excess. Bake one side until top is dry and starts to blister. Turn out onto board. Fill with 1 tablespoon of filling. Roll and fold in sides. Refrigerate or freeze. When ready to serve, brush tops with melted butter. Bake at 400° F for ½ hour. Serve with sour cream, blueberries, etc.

Chafing-Dish Meatballs

*#2   50–60 *meatballs*

Probably the most popular hors d'oeuvres in the book.
Combine

2 lbs ground meat	1 large grated onion
1 slightly beaten egg	Salt to taste

Mix and shape into small balls. Drop into sauce of:

1 twelve-oz bottle chili sauce	Juice of 1 lemon
1 ten-oz jar grape jelly	

Simmer until brown. Refrigerate or freeze. To serve bring to room temperature. Reheat in chafing dish and serve with cocktail picks.

Cheddar Straws

*#1   6 *dozen*

Excellent with hot soup, aperitifs, or cold salads.
Sift together

1½ cups flour, sifted	¼ teaspoon dry mustard
1 teaspoon seasoned salt	

Cut in

½ cup butter

with pastry blender (preferably fingers), until it resembles corn meal.

Sprinkle over mixture

3–3½ tablespoons water

Work until it forms a ball. Turn out on floured board; role into rectangle ¼ inch thick. Sprinkle half the surface with

⅓ cup shredded cheddar cheese	**1 teaspoon paprika**

Fold plain half onto covered surface; pinch edges to seal. Roll out to rectangle. Sprinkle with

⅓ cup cheddar cheese	**1 teaspoon paprika**

Repeat folding and sprinkling and folding. Roll into rectangle. Cut into strips ½ inch wide and 3 inches long. Place on ungreased cookie sheet. Bake at 425° F 10–12 minutes or until slightly puffed and golden. Cool on wire racks.

Dip one end in

Paprika

Refrigerate or freeze. Refresh in 350° F oven before serving.

Cheese and Mushroom Canapés

*#2   2½ *dozen*

So easy and simply delicious!

Slice in tiny pieces

¼ lb mushrooms

Cook for a few minutes in

1 tablespoon butter

Mix mushrooms with

1 eight-oz package cream cheese	**Salt**
	Pepper
1 teaspoon minced onion	**Add enough cream to soften**

Toast on one side

Small rounds of bread

Spread the untoasted side with

Butter   **Mushroom mixture**

Refrigerate or freeze. When ready to serve, place under broiler until puffy and brown.

Cheese Shorties

*#3   *4 dozen*

Cream until fluffy

**1 lb sharp cheddar cheese,   ½ lb butter
grated**

Add

2 cups sifted flour   ½ teaspoon garlic salt

Make into rolls 1 inch in diameter and wrap in waxed paper. Chill or freeze. To serve, cut into ⅓-inch slices. Place on cookie sheet 1 inch apart. Bake at 400° F for 10 minutes.

Cheese Tarts, Miniature

*#1   *about 2 dozen*

Prepare

1 pie crust recipe

Roll out into rectangle same thickness as for pie crust. Cut into 2-inch squares. Press each square into 1-inch muffin cups.

Beat together thoroughly (with egg beater)

3 eggs   ¼ cup sour cream

Stir in

**¼ lb finely grated Swiss   ¼ teaspoon poppy seeds
cheese   ⅛ teaspoon pepper
½ teaspoon grated onion**

Place on bottom of each unbaked tart shell

Small piece crisp bacon

Fill tarts with cheese mixture. Refrigerate or freeze. When ready to serve bring to room temperature and bake tarts at 425° F for 5 minutes. Reduce oven to 325° F and bake 12 minutes longer, until brown.

Clam-Tomato Dip

*#2
Combine

2 six-oz cans tomato paste
2 ten and a half-oz cans minced clams, drained
1 teaspoon oregano

2 cloves garlic, cut up and browned in olive oil
2–4 teaspoons flour

Refrigerate or freeze. When ready to serve, heat and place in chafing dish. Serve with crackers as dippers.

Clams Casino

*#1   5 dozen
In water almost to cover, boil until they open
4 dozen cleaned little-neck clams
Remove meat from shells, saving
1 cup clam broth
Put clams through meat grinder with
2 hard-boiled eggs
Sauté until golden
6 large chopped onions
in
½ cup butter
Add clams and eggs to onions. Then add
1 cup bread crumbs
Mix to pasty consistency. Add enough
Clam juice to moisten
Stuff mixture in clam shells. Refrigerate or freeze. When ready to serve, cover each shell with
¼ strip of bacon
Refrigerate or freeze. To serve broil until bacon is brown, about 15 minutes.

Crabmeat Canapés

*#2   4 dozen
Whip together
6 oz cream cheese   ¼ cup heavy cream

Beat in

¼ cup mayonnaise

Add

1 teaspoon minced onion   ½ clove garlic, mashed

½ teaspoon minced chives   Pinch salt

Marinate for 1 hour in

¼ cup lemon juice   ½ lb crabmeat

Drain. Fold into sauce. Add

⅛ teaspoon Worcestershire   2 drops hot pepper sauce
sauce

Refrigerate or freeze. To serve put on crackers and broil a few minutes, until lightly browned. Serve hot.

Crabmeat Crêpes

about 30 pieces

A true French delight. This is an authentic recipe and can be used for Crêpes Suzette, etc.

CRÊPES BATTER (*#7)

Put in a small bowl

4 heaping tablespoons flour   1 tablespoon vegetable oil

1 whole egg   3 tablespoons milk

1 egg yolk

Stir with wire whisk until quite smooth.

Use enough from

1 cup milk

to make thin, creamlike consistency. Put in refrigerator for 3 or 4 hours. (It may be kept in refrigerator up to a week.) Remove and add enough of rest of milk to reduce to thin consistency again. Heat 6- or 7-inch frying pan; when very hot wipe out with piece of buttered waxed paper. Return to lowered heat. Cover bottom of pan with very thin layer of batter (pour off any excess). Cook until golden on one side; turn and cook on other side until golden. Stack them as they are cooked.

Spread crabmeat mixture on each crêpe. Roll like cylinder.

Cut into 3 pieces. Refrigerate or freeze. When ready to serve, defrost, heat in top of double boiler. Serve from chafing dish.

CRABMEAT FILLING (* #1)

Melt

2 tablespoons butter

Remove from fire and stir in

2 tablespoons flour

Stir in carefully

½ cup milk   **½ cup vegetable stock (can be made with vegetable bouillon cube)**

Cook, stirring until smooth and boiling. Season with

Salt   **Paprika**

Sauté

6 shallots, finely chopped

in

3 tablespoons butter

Add

½ lb crabmeat

Add to sauce

2 beaten egg yolks   **1 tablespoon chives, finely chopped**
1 tablespoon Madeira

Combination mixtures. Cool before filling crêpes.

Crabmeat Quiche

*#1   *8 servings*

Excellent! Lois' mother's best recipe.

CRUST

Sift together

1 cup flour   **⅛ teaspoon salt**
1 tablespoon sugar   **1 teaspoon baking powder**

Blend in

¼ lb butter

Mix thoroughly through hands until sugar is dissolved. If necessary add a few drops of water (not more than a teaspoon) to get a rolling consistency. Roll between waxed paper and line a 10-inch pie plate.

FILLING

Line unbaked pie shell with
½ lb Swiss cheese cut in slices ¼ inch thick
Cover with layer of

1 cup crabmeat   **½ cup small cooked shrimp**
Combine

1½ cups light cream   **Dash of pepper**
4 eggs, beaten   **Dash of cayenne**
1 tablespoon flour   **¼ teaspoon nutmeg**
½ teaspoon salt
Stir in

2 tablespoons melted butter   **2 tablespoons dry sherry**

Beat well. Pour over seafood. Refrigerate or freeze. When ready to serve bring to room temperature and bake at 375° F for 40 minutes or until browned. Let stand for 20 minutes before serving.

Cream Puffs

*#2   *50–60 miniature*
One of the most elegant and impressive of hors d'oeuvres.

SHELLS

Heat oven to 400° F. Bring to boil in a 2-quart pot
1 cup water   **½ cup butter**
Reduce heat to low. Add

½ teaspoon salt   **1 cup sifted all purpose flour**

Cook, stirring vigorously until mixture leaves sides of pot and forms compact ball. Remove from heat. Cool slightly. Add one at a time, beating well after each addition
4 eggs

Drop by half-teaspoonfuls on ungreased cookie sheet and bake about 30 minutes until light and dry. When ready to use, cut off tops and fill with one of the following:

CREAM CHEESE AND HAM (* #3)

Combine

6 oz cream cheese   Catsup to moisten
1 three-oz can deviled ham

CREAM CHEESE AND ROQUEFORT (* #3)

Combine

3 oz cream cheese   Dry sherry to moisten
Roquefort to taste

SHRIMP SOUP (#1)

Let thaw completely

1 ten and one-quarter-oz can frozen shrimp soup
Add
2 heaping tablespoons sour cream

TONGUE (#1)

Melt

¼ lb butter
Add and stir until blended
½ cup flour
Gradually add
1½ cups milk
Cook over moderate heat until thickened; stirring constantly.
Stir in

1 cup cottage cheese   ½ teaspoon basil
¼ lb tongue, finely diced   ¼ teaspoon pepper
1 five-oz can water chest-   ½ teaspoon salt
    nuts, diced

Fill 1-inch cream puffs with choice of mixtures. Replace tops. When ready to serve heat at 425° F.

Ham and Cheese Dip

* #2

Melt over low heat
1 lb cheddar cheese

Stir in

2 **four and a half-oz cans deviled ham**
2 **teaspoons mustard**
2 **teaspoons Worcestershire sauce**

Refrigerate or freeze. When ready to serve, heat and serve from chafing dish, with crackers as dippers.

Horseradish Meatballs
*#1   5 *dozen*

Mix together and shape into 1-inch balls

½ **cup water**   1 **cup water chestnuts,**
1 **egg**   **chopped**
½ **cup bread crumbs**   1 **lb ground chuck**
2 **tablespoons prepared**
horseradish

Bake 10 minutes in a shallow roasting pan at 350° F uncovered. When cool, cover with foil and freeze. When ready to serve bake for 15 minutes covered at 350° F then broil until brown. Serve with Marmalade Dip.

DIP

Combine and heat

⅓ **cup orange marmalade**   2 **tablespoons lemon juice**
1 **clove garlic, minced**   ⅓ **cup water**
¼ **cup soy sauce**

Serve hot.

Meat-Filled Mushroom Caps
*#1   2 *dozen*

Remove stems from

2 **dozen large mushrooms**

Marinate caps for 1 hour in

½ **cup soy sauce**

Finely chop stems and mix with

½ **lb ground beef**   1 **tablespoon minced onion**
¼ **cup minced green pepper** ½ **clove garlic**
2 **tablespoons bread crumbs** ¼ **teaspoon salt**
1 **egg yolk**   ¼ **teaspoon pepper**

Drain caps. Stuff with meat mixture mounded high. Brush tops with soy sauce. Broil 8–10 minutes. Refrigerate or freeze. When ready to serve, bring to room temperature and bake at 350° F for 8–10 minutes.

Olive-Cheese Nuggets

*#2   35 *pieces*

Shred
¼ lb sharp cheddar cheese
Blend with

¼ cup soft butter	**⅛ teaspoon salt**
¾ cup sifted flour	**½ teaspoon paprika**

Mix to form dough. Shape 1 teaspoon of dough around each of
35 small, stuffed green olives
Refrigerate or freeze. When ready to serve, bring to room temperature and place on ungreased baking sheet. Bake at 400° F for 12–15 minutes.

Oysters Rockefeller

*#1

Allow 4–6 oysters on half shell per person.
Place in each shell
1 teaspoon cooked chopped spinach
Place on top of that the oyster, then top each oyster with

Butter creamed with onion juice	**Cooked bacon, minced**
	Dash of cayenne
Chopped parsley	**Bread crumbs**
Salt	**Dot of Butter**

Freeze or refrigerate. To serve return to room temperature and bake at 450° F to 500° F for 10 minutes or until oysters are plump and brown.

Sherley's Parmesan Puffs

#1

They disappear like soap bubbles.

Mix to a consistency of softened butter

Mayonnaise   Parmesan cheese, freshly
                                grated

Place in center of

Rounds of white bread, 1   About ⅛ teaspoon chopped
inch in diameter   onion

Cover bread round completely with

Mayonnaise-cheese mixture

Refrigerate if desired. To serve broil about 5–8 minutes until puffed and brown. Serve immediately.

Pizzas, Miniature

*#2   *3 dozen*

You can never serve enough!

Spread

1 loaf party rye

with ingredients in order:

Tomato paste   Slice of Mozzarella cheese
Thin slice of salami   Dash of oregano

Refrigerate or freeze. When ready to serve, toast under broiler until cheese is melted and beginning to brown.

Potato Pancakes, Miniature

*#1

Grate

4 very large potatoes

Drain off half of liquid. Add

2 beaten eggs   2 teaspoons onion, grated
1 teaspoon salt   ½ teaspoon baking powder
1 tablespoon flour

Mix well. Drop by teaspoonful onto hot greased skillet. Brown well on both sides. Refrigerate or freeze. When ready to serve, reheat in 450° F oven until very crispy. Serve with sour cream. To freeze or refrigerate, place between sheets of aluminum foil, or they will become soggy.

Ramaki

*#1   *80–90 hors d'oeuvres*

Cut in half
1 lb bacon, extra thin slices
Cut in quarters
2 five-oz cans water chestnuts
Cut in half
2 lbs chicken livers
Wrap piece of bacon around water chestnut and chicken liver. Fasten with toothpick. Marinate them for two hours in

1 cup soy sauce   **½ cup brown sugar**

Drain and broil 3–4 minutes on each side, until bacon is not quite crisp. Remove toothpicks and freeze or refrigerate. When ready to serve, bring to room temperature and reheat in 400° F oven until bacon is really crisp.

Refrigerator Cheese Rolls

*#2   *3 dozen*

Grate
½ lb aged cheddar cheese
Add

3 tablespoons mayonnaise   **2 teaspoons Worcestershire**
1 tablespoon soft butter   **sauce**
                                    ½ teaspoon garlic salt

Remove crusts from
1 loaf sliced, fresh white bread
Roll thin. Spread mixture on bread. Roll up. Refrigerate or freeze. To serve return to room temperature; slice each roll in half. Broil until lightly browned.

Sesame Wafers

*#2   *about 3 dozen*

Cream

½ cup butter   4 oz cream cheese

Add

1 cup flour, sifted

Mix until smooth. Chill. Roll out on lightly floured board and cut into rounds—about 1 inch in diameter. Brush top of each with

Lightly beaten egg

Sprinkle with

Sesame seeds

Bake at 425° F 12–15 minutes. Refrigerate or freeze. Heat at 350° F to refresh at serving time.

Shrimp and Bacon

*#1   *60 hors d'oeuvres*

Marinate

3 lbs shrimp, raw, peeled and deveined

in

1 twelve-oz bottle chili sauce   2 cloves garlic

Wrap each shrimp in

Extra thin, sliced bacon, partially cooked

Freeze or refrigerate. When ready to serve, bring to room temperature and broil turning to brown evenly.

Shrimp and Cheese Nibblings
NIBBLINGS (#1)

2 lbs raw shrimp, shelled and   1 lb Swiss cheese, cubed
  deveined   1 can pitted ripe olives

SAUCE (#3)

Sauté until crisp

4 slices bacon, cut in small pieces

Add and simmer to thickened mixture

4 tablespoons butter
1½ teaspoons garlic salt
1 cup tomato paste
1 cup tomato juice
½ cup water

⅛ teaspoon dried basil
⅛ teaspoon oregano
⅛ teaspoon marjoram
½ cup dry red wine

Add

3 tablespoons lemon juice

Adjust seasonings. When ready to serve, heat sauce. Pour sauce into chafing dish, add shrimp, and cook until pink. Add cheese, olives. Serve with cocktail picks.

Spicy Sausage Balls

*#2   4 *dozen*

Mix together

1 lb spicy sausage meat
1 slightly beaten egg

⅓ cup seasoned bread crumbs
½ teaspoon sage

Shape into about 4 dozen balls. Brown them in skillet on all sides. Pour off grease.

Combine and add to meatballs

½ cup catsup and chili sauce combined
2 tablespoons brown sugar

1 tablespoon vinegar
1 tablespoon soy sauce

Cover and simmer 30 minutes. Refrigerate or freeze. When ready to serve, reheat, place in chafing dish, and serve with cocktail picks.

Sweet-and-Sour Franks

*#3   60–80 *pieces*

Mix

¾ cup prepared mustard   1 cup currant jelly

Place in top of double boiler.

Slice diagonally, ½ inch thick

2 lbs frankfurters

Add to sauce and cook for 5 minutes. Refrigerate or freeze. When ready to serve, place in chafing dish and heat. Serve with cocktail picks.

Swiss Fondue

#1

A rather hearty hors d'oeuvre and quite appropriate for a late supper. It has its own rules: Do not use a metal chafing dish. Spear cubes of bread and dip into the bubbling pot, stirring gently to keep the fondue blended. Lift out with twirling motion so you won't lose any of the cheese.

Cut into bite-sized pieces, giving each one a crusty side
1 one-lb loaf French bread
Shred
1 lb imported Swiss cheese
Mix together and set aside
2 tablespoons cornstarch   2 tablespoons kirsch
Rub the chafing dish with cut surface of
1 clove garlic
Put into the chafing dish shredded cheese and mixture of
¼ teaspoon salt   ⅛ teaspoon pepper
¼ teaspoon MSG
Refrigerate. At serving time pour over this mixture
2 cups Neuchâtel wine
When cheese is melted blend in
Cornstarch mixture
Stir until bubbly. Guests start dipping when fondue bubbles.

Toasted Mushroom Rolls

*#3   3½ dozen
Guests vie to see who can eat the most.

PLAIN

Clean and chop fine
½ lb mushrooms

Sauté for five minutes in
¼ **cup butter**
Blend in

3 **tablespoons flour**   ¼ **teaspoon MSG**
¾ **teaspoon salt**
Stir in
1 **cup light cream**
Cook until thick. Add

2 **teaspoons minced chives**   1 **teaspoon lemon juice**
Cool. Remove crust from
1 **family-sized loaf sliced, fresh white bread**
Roll slices thin. Spread with mixture, roll up. Pack and freeze, if desired. When ready to serve, defrost, cut each roll in half, and toast on all sides in 400° F oven.

WITH LOBSTER

6 dozen

Add to Mushroom Mixture
1 **lb lobster meat, minced**
Follow directions for bread, using 2 regular-sized loaves. Fill and roll. When ready to serve, slice in half, follow directions for plain rolls.

Cold Hors D'oeuvres

ABC Chip Dip

#3

Combine and mix lightly

⅓ cup toasted, chopped almonds

3 strips cooked bacon, crumbled

¾ cup mayonnaise

1½ cups sharp cheddar cheese, grated

1 tablespoon finely minced onion

¼ teaspoon salt

Serve with shredded wheat crackers.

Avocado and Bleu-Cheese Dip

#1

½ cup

Peel and mash

1 avocado

Add to purée

¼ cup mashed bleu cheese

Stir in

1 tablespoon lemon juice

Season with

Salt   **Pepper**

Chill and serve with crackers.

Bleu-Cheese Almond Spread

#3   *2 cups*

Mash

4 oz bleu cheese

Blend in

½ cup crumbled soft ched-   **1 tablespoon Worcestershire**
dar cheese   **sauce**
1 cup sour cream   **1 teaspoon paprika**

Add

½ cup toasted, slivered almonds

Spread on biscuits, toast.

Camembert Glacé

*#3   *12 servings*

Remove skin from

4 canned Camembert cheeses (four and a half oz total)

Mix with

½ lb butter

Pat back into shape and roll in

Bread crumbs

Place back in cans. Refrigerate or freeze. Serve at room
temperature with toast or French bread slices.

Caviar Mold

#2   *fills 2-cup mold*

A little caviar can go a long way.
Blend until smooth

1 cup sour cream
1 cup creamed cottage
cheese
1 clove garlic, crushed
¼ teaspoon seasoning salt
1 teaspoon Worcestershire
sauce

A dash each of soy sauce,
hot pepper sauce, celery
salt, garlic salt, onion salt,
black pepper, cayenne, paprika, and chili powder

Soften
1 envelope gelatin
in
¼ cup dry sherry
Place in pan and stir over low heat until granules disappear. Do not boil! Add gelatin to blender and whip. Pour
into lightly greased 1-pint mold and refrigerate until firm.
When ready to serve, unmold and top with
Caviar mixed with juice of ½ lemon
Note: If you use a heart-shaped mold, it will look like the
classic "coeur à la crème."

Cheddar-Cheese Balls

#1   *30 balls*
½ lb cheddar cheese
(If you use the soft variety, roll into balls. If you use the
hard type, cut into balls with melon-ball cutter.)
Chop separately until very fine

8 radishes   Sprigs of parsley
1 carrot
Roll about 10 balls in each kind of mixture.

Cheese-Almond Slices

*#2   40 *pieces*

Sauté until golden, then chop fine
1 **cup blanched almonds
in 3 tablespoons butter**

Cream together
3 **oz cream cheese**   ½ **lb sharp cheddar cheese,
                            grated**

Add almonds to cheese. Then add
1 **pimiento, chopped**   1 **teaspoon Worcestershire**
1 **tablespoon lemon juice**   **sauce**
1½ **teaspoons salt**   1 **teaspoon grated onion
                            Dash paprika**

Mix well. Shape into roll. Roll in
Chopped toasted almonds

Wrap in waxed paper. Refrigerate or freeze. To serve, defrost and cut into thin slices and serve with crackers.

Cheese Biscuits

#3   5 *dozen*

In a tin can these will keep 3 or 4 weeks.

Combine thoroughly until completely blended (use your fingers)
1 **lb flour, sifted**   1 **lb finely grated, sharp**
1 **lb softened butter**   **cracker-barrel cheese**

Divide into 5 or 6 portions and shape into cylinders about 1-inch in diameter. Chill for 2 hours and slice into ¼-inch slices and place on ungreased cookie sheet. Bake at 400° F 10–12 minutes. Remove immediately from baking sheet.

Chive-Anchovy Spread

#3   ½ cup

Mix

8 oz chive cream cheese   1 can rolled anchovies
1½ pimientos cut up fine

Refrigerate. Serve with crackers.

Chopped Liver

#2

Sauté

1 medium onion, finely chopped
in chicken fat or butter

Add

1 lb chicken livers

Sauté until just slightly pink inside. Season with salt and
pepper. Put through meat grinder, using small blade, with

1 small raw onion   1 hard-boiled egg

Add

Chicken fat

to make moist. (This mixture may be served on crisp
greens or placed in a decorative oiled mold. To remove, place
mold for a few seconds in hot water and invert.)

Serve with party rye or crackers.

Chive-Cheese Spread

#2

Mix

1 eight-oz package cottage   Sour cream to soften
  cheese with chives   1 teaspoon onion salt
1 four-oz package cream   1 teaspoon garlic salt
  cheese with chives   ½ teaspoon oregano
2 heaping tablespoons may-   Dash Worcestershire sauce
  onnaise

Refrigerate. Serve with crackers or party rye.

Clam Dip

#2

Drain, reserving juice

1 ten and a half-oz can minced clams

Combine clams with

6 oz cream cheese

2 teaspoons grated onion

¼ teaspoon hot pepper
sauce

⅛ teaspoon Worcestershire
sauce

¼ teaspoon lemon juice

½ teaspoon clam juice

Blend thoroughly. Chill. Serve with crackers or bread rounds.

Cold-Cut Slices

#3

Cut ends off and remove soft crumbs from

3 very narrow, long French rolls

Brush insides with

Prepared mustard

Mash

6 slices liverwurst

12 slices garlic salami

2 hard-boiled eggs

2 tablespoons grated Swiss
cheese

Blend with

1 tablespoon each of
chopped parsley, chives,
grated onion

2 cloves garlic, minced

Add enough

Mayonnaise

to spread well and

2 teaspoons Worcestershire sauce

Fill rolls. Chill thoroughly. Slice thinly.

Crab and Clam Dip

#1
Blend

6 oz cream cheese   ¼ cup French dressing
4 tablespoons soft butter
Add

1 ten and a half-oz can   Eight-oz can shredded crab-
drained minced clams   meat
Mix lightly. Season to taste with
Worcestershire sauce   Hot pepper sauce
Refrigerate. Serve with crackers. (This can also be spread
on toasted rye and placed under broiler until bubbly.)

Curried Cheese Roll

*#3
Put through meat grinder alternately

1 lb sharp cheddar cheese   1 clove garlic
1 cup pecans, unsalted   Dash cayenne pepper
1 three-oz package cream
cheese
Thoroughly mix. Roll into 1-inch cylinders. Roll in
Curry powder
Wrap waxed paper around rolls. Refrigerate at least 2 hours.
Let guests slice and spread on rye rounds.

Curried Chicken Balls

*#1   5 dozen
Something different for leftover chicken.
Thoroughly cream

½ lb cream cheese   4 tablespoons mayonnaise
Add

2 cups cooked chicken,   3 tablespoons chutney,
chopped   chopped
1½ cups blanched almonds,   1 teaspoon salt
chopped   2 teaspoons curry powder

Shape into walnut-sized balls. Roll each ball in
1 cup grated coconut
Chill until ready to serve.

Curry Almond Spread

*#3   *2 cups*

Mix together

16 oz soft cream cheese   **½ teaspoon dry mustard**
½ cup chopped chutney   **½ cup toasted chopped al-**
2 teaspoons curry powder   **monds**

Refrigerate for several hours, at least. Spread on party rye
or crackers.

Fruit-of-the-Sea Dip

#3   *3½ to 4 cups*
*Improves upon standing . . . prepare at least a day in
advance.*
Combine

1 cup mayonnaise   **1½ tablespoons lemon juice**
6 tablespoons chili sauce   **2 tablespoons pickle relish**
1 teaspoon grated onion   **2 tablespoons catsup**
1 tablespoon Worcestershire   **2 tablespoons heavy cream**
sauce

Add

1 lb finely cut-up, cooked shrimp
Serve with crackers, potato chips.

Green Onion Dip

#2   *1 pint*
A quickie, quickie . . .
Mix together

1 pint sour cream   **1 envelope green onion dip**
Refrigerate. Serve with potato chips or crackers.

Mare's Cheese-Egg Dip

#2
Soften
1 three-oz package chive cream cheese
Stir in

2 tablespoons mayonnaise   ⅛ teaspoon pepper
1 teaspoon prepared   1 teaspoon Worcestershire
  mustard   sauce
¼ teaspoon salt
Add
2 hard-boiled eggs, well chopped
Gradually beat in
2 to 4 tablespoons milk
Refrigerate until ½ hour before serving.
Sprinkle with
Paprika
Serve with crackers, potato chips.

Mystery Cheese Ball

*#3   *3–5 balls*
Will feed an army.
Leave at room temperature and then whirl in the electric
mixer

2 lbs Old English cheese   8 oz package cream cheese
5 oz jar bleu cheese spread
Mix, then roll into 3 or 4 large balls. Roll each ball in
Chopped walnuts or pecans
Refrigerate or freeze. Serve at room temperature with
crackers.

Mystery Spread

#3
Try this one—an unbelievable combination.
Put through grinder

1 three-oz can pimiento   1 seven-oz can salted peanuts

Mix with

1 **tablespoon mayonnaise**

Refrigerate at least 2 hours. Serve with crackers.

Pâté de Maison

#3   *one 9x5″ loaf*

The real McCoy and very easy to put together.

Mix together

2 **lbs calf's liver, uncooked,**   2 **lbs sausage meat, well sea-**
  ground   **soned, uncooked**
                                      Plenty of salt and pepper

Grease well a 9x5-inch loaf mold (same as bread pan).
Line it with

Uncooked bacon

Have slices touching each other but not overlapping. Fill
mold with half the meat mixture.

Cut lengthwise

2 **hard-boiled eggs**

Arrange down center of mold. Place on top in latticework
design julienned slices of

6 **oz liverwurst sausage**   6 **whole chicken livers, un-**
6 **oz cooked ham**   **cooked**
6 **oz cooked tongue**

Cover with rest of meat mixture and fold over ends of
the bacon slices. Cover the whole with waxed paper. Put the
mold in a pan of water and bake for 1½ hours in a 350° F
oven. Remove from oven and water; weight pâté with heavy
object. Cool and refrigerate. To serve, unmold on bed of
greens, cut in thin slices and serve with Melba toast.

Pâté en Gelee

#2   *fills 1½-quart mold*

Will fool the most discriminating gourmet . . .

Mix together

2 cans liver pâté   6 oz cream cheese
1 four and a half-oz can   Worcestershire sauce to
   deviled ham   taste

Dissolve

1 envelope gelatin
in
½ cup cold water

Add gelatin to

1 cup beef consomme   ¼ cup dry sherry

which have been heated together. Pour small amount gelatin
mixture into bottom of 1½-quart mold. When almost set
arrange on bottom

Sliced stuffed olives

Pour remaining gelatin mixture into mold. Let it set. Put
pâté mixture on top. Refrigerate. When ready to serve, unmold and serve with party rye or crackers.

Pickled Shrimp

#7   *about 4 dozen shrimp*

Marvelous and low calorie too.

Combine and mix well

1¼ cup salad oil   2½ tablespoons capers and
¾ cup vinegar   juice
1½ teaspoons salt   Dash hot pepper sauce
2½ teaspoons celery seed

Pour sauce over

2 lbs shrimp, cooked and cleaned

Place in shallow dish in which the shrimp may be served.
Cover with

1 onion, thinly sliced in rings

Add

2–3 bay leaves

Cover and store in refrigerator at least 24 hours. Drain and serve. Will keep 1 week in refrigerator.

Pickles and Peanuts

#3

Crazy but good.

Whip together

1 eight-oz package cream cheese

½ cup salted peanuts, chopped *very fine*

½ cup chopped sweet gherkins

1 teaspoon seasoned salt

1 teaspoon minced parsley

Put into crocks ready to serve. Refrigerate. Serve with crackers.

Plaza Dip

#2

Blend together and chill at least 2 hours

1½ cups sour cream
½ cup mayonnaise
1 teaspoon dry mustard
1 tablespoon horseradish
1 clove garlic, crushed
2 tablespoons chili sauce

2 tablespoons anchovy paste
2 hard-boiled eggs, chopped
1 green pepper, chopped
1 tablespoon chopped parsley

Serve with chips or crackers.

Raw Vegetables with Dip

#1

For the diet-conscious.

Clean, cut up, and wrap securely

Carrot sticks
Raw cauliflowerettes

Radish roses
Cucumber sticks

DIP (#2)

Mix together

1 pint sour cream	1 teaspoon salt
1⅓ tablespoons white horse- radish	1 teaspoon tarragon
	¼ teaspoon MSG
1 tablespoon paprika	1 clove garlic, crushed
1 tablespoon minced chives	⅛ teaspoon pepper

Chill thoroughly. Surround bowl with vegetables.

Shrimp Cocktail Sauce

#1   *1 cup, 6 servings*

Foolproof sauce.

Combine

⅓ cup chili sauce	2 teaspoons Worcestershire
⅓ cup catsup	sauce
3 tablespoons horseradish	Dash salt
4 tablespoons lemon juice	Dash hot pepper sauce

When ready to serve, divide

1 lb cooked shrimp

into 6 servings and place on crisp lettuce leaves. Spoon sauce over all.

Shrimp Mix

#1

Blend together

8 oz cream cheese	8 tablespoons mayonnaise

Mix in

2 tablespoons Worcester- shire sauce	½ lb cut-up cooked shrimp (1 teaspoon red horseradish,
2 tablespoons onion juice	if desired)
2 diced fresh tomatoes	

Refrigerate. Serve with crackers or chips.

Smoked Salmon Pinwheels

*#1   *30 hors d'oeuvres*

Spread

8 oz cream cheese

on

½ lb of large thin slices of smoked salmon

Roll up. Refrigerate or freeze. Slice and serve on Melba toast rounds.

Smokey Cheese

#1

A *quickie.*

Combine thoroughly

1 six-oz package smoked cheese spread	**3 tablespoons sparerib sauce**

Serve on crackers.

Stix and Stones

*#7   *6 quarts*

In a large roasting pan mix together

1 six-oz package small cheese crackers	**1 eight-oz can walnuts**
2 six-oz packages corn chips	**2 six-oz cans pecans**
2 four-oz cans toasted coconut chips	**1 three and a half-oz package popcorn**

Mix together in saucepan

½ lb melted butter	**1 teaspoon curry powder**
½ teaspoon garlic salt	**6 drops hot pepper sauce**
1 clove garlic, crushed	**1 tablespoon Worcestershire sauce**
1 teaspoon salt	

Sprinkle liquid mixture through dry mixture. Bake at 250° F for 1 hour, stirring occasionally. This may be made weeks in advance if stored in airtight containers.

Stuffed Rigatoni

#1   *30 hors d'oeuvres*

Cook according to directions on package

30 large rigatoni

Blend

1 three-oz can deviled ham   **2 tablespoons mayonnaise**
**1 five-oz jar pimiento cheese
spread**

Fill each rigatoni with mixture. Insert

Stuffed olives

into one end of each rigatoni. Refrigerate.

Tuna-Cheese Spread

#3

Try it hot too!

Cut into pieces and melt in top of double boiler

1 eight-oz package processed Old English cheese

Remove from heat and add

1 seven-oz can tuna fish   **½ teaspoon Worcestershire**
½ cup mayonnaise   **sauce**

Chill. Serve with crackers.

II : Elegant but Easy
Main Dishes

Meat

Beef and Onions—Chinese

#1   *4 servings*

Do not overcook any vegetables in Chinese cooking (or for that matter, ever!).

Heat

2 tablespoons oil (preferably peanut)

Sauté in oil very slightly

3 cups onion rings, thinly sliced

Add

2 tablespoons soy sauce   2 teaspoons dry sherry

½ teaspoon sugar

Continue to heat a few seconds. Remove from pan.

Dredge

1 lb top round beefsteak, sliced very fine

in mixture of

4 teaspoons cornstarch	2 teaspoons dry sherry
2 tablespoons soy sauce	

Heat pan and add

4 tablespoons oil (preferably peanut)

Sauté beef until browned. Remove from fire. Add onions and refrigerate. When ready to serve reheat.

Beef Roulades

*#2   4 serving

A gourmet's delight!

BATTER

Mix and sift

1 cup flour, sifted	Dash salt
1 tablespoon sugar	

Beat and add to dry ingredients

3 eggs

Add and stir until smooth

1 cup milk

Add

2 tablespoons melted butter

Strain through fine sieve. Let stand at least three hours or overnight. Wipe heated 6-inch or 7-inch frying pan with buttered wax paper. Pour in about 3 tablespoons batter, pouring off any excess. When set and brown on underside, turn and brown other side. Repeat entire process making at least 8 very thin pancakes.

FILLING

Brown

¾ lb ground chuck, round, etc.	½ lb mushrooms, finely chopped
1 medium onion, finely chopped	

in

2 tablespoons butter

Add

½ teaspoon salt

Dash pepper

  Simmer 5 minutes. Add

½ cup catsup

1 tablespoon bottled steak
sauce

1 teaspoon parsley, snipped

1 teaspoon oregano

¼ teaspoon rosemary

1 teaspoon dry mustard

2 garlic cloves, minced

1 bay leaf, crumbled

2 cups cheddar cheese,
coarsely crumbled

½ cup Parmesan cheese,
shredded

Cover and simmer until cheese is almost all melted. Remove from heat. Spread beef mixture on pancakes. Fold in two sides and roll up. Place in greased baking dish. Sprinkle with

½ cup Parmesan cheese, shredded

  Using

16 slices mozzarella cheese

place 2 on each roll. Sprinkle with

Paprika

Refrigerate or freeze. When ready to serve bring to room temperature, pour over

½ cup dry sherry

Bake at 350° F for 30 minutes. Mozzarella should be melted and browned.

Blanquette de Veau

*#2   6 *servings*

  A *French classic.*

  Simmer in deep covered pot for 1 hour or until tender

2 lbs boned veal shoulder, cut in 1¼-inch pieces

with

1 quart boiling water

5 medium carrots, scraped
and quartered

4 whole cloves, stuck in
1 small onion

1 bay leaf

⅛ teaspoon thyme

2 sprigs parsley

½ cup thinly sliced celery

4 peppercorns

1 tablespoon salt

Drain and reserve 3½ cups stock.
Melt

¼ cup butter

Add

15 small white onions (about 1 lb)

Cover and simmer 30 minutes. Add onions to drained veal.
In same skillet cook for 15 minutes

½ lb small, fresh mushrooms

in

½ cup veal stock

Add veal and onions.
Melt

2 tablespoons butter

Remove from fire and add

¼ cup flour

Slowly add, constantly stirring

3 cups veal stock

Cook, stirring, over medium heat until thickened and boiling. Whisk slightly

2 egg yolks   **2 tablespoons lemon juice**

Slowly whisk in a little hot sauce. Then return all to rest of sauce. Combine veal and sauce.

Refrigerate or freeze. When ready to serve, heat but do not boil. Make a ring of rice or fluffy mashed potatoes and place veal in center. Sprinkle on

2 teaspoons or more snipped fresh dill

Boeuf Bourguignonne

*#2   *4–6 servings*

Combine in large casserole

2 lbs cubed beef (chuck, round steak, etc.)

3–4 carrots, cut up

1 cup chopped celery

2 onions, sliced

2 cups canned tomatoes

1 cup tomato sauce

1 clove garlic

3 tablespoons quick cooking tapioca

1 tablespoon sugar

½ cup red Burgundy

Cook at 250° F for 5 hours. During last hour add

1 cup sliced water chestnuts	2 one-lb cans small Irish po-
1 six-oz can mushrooms	tatoes

After four hours of cooking, freeze, if desired. To serve, defrost and cook at 250° F for 1 hour, adding water chestnuts, mushrooms, and potatoes.

Carbonnade of Beef

#2   10 *servings*

Overnight marinate

1½ cups dried prunes	1½ cups dried apricots

in

1½ cups beer	½ teaspoon ground ginger

Sprinkle with salt and allow to stand 1 hour

6 lb boneless fresh brisket of beef

In large Dutch oven or heavy pot brown beef on all sides in own fat. Add and brown

2 onions, sliced

Add

¼ cup water

Simmer 1 hour. Cool. Remove meat from stock and slice. Skim fat off meat. Return meat to stock with

½ teaspoon cinnamon	⅓ cup honey
Dash pepper	½ cup brown sugar

Simmer 1 hour, covered. Add

10 medium potatoes, thinly sliced	1½ cups dried prunes 1½ cups dried apricots

Pour in marinade. Simmer, covered, about 30 minutes more. Refrigerate. When ready to serve, reheat. Place meat slices down middle of platter and arrange potatoes and fruit around edges.

Chili Con Carne

*#2   4 *servings*

Brown in small amount

Cooking oil	**2 onions, chopped**

Add and brown
1½ lbs ground chuck
Add

1 ten and a half-oz can to-mato soup	**½ of 1 lb can kidney beans, mashed**
1 lb can tomatoes	

Simmer 1 hour.
Add

Rest of kidney beans, whole   1 teaspoon chili powder

Simmer 5 minutes more. Refrigerate or freeze. When ready to serve, reheat and serve on spaghetti or macaroni shells.

Chinese Beef

#1   6 *servings*

Cut into thin strips across the grain
1 flank steak
Cut up and set aside

2 fresh tomatoes, quartered	**2 green peppers, ribs and seeds removed, cut in chunks**

Heat in skillet
2 tablespoons salad oil
Add beef and brown on all sides with

1 clove garlic	**Dash pepper**
1 teaspoon salt	**¼ teaspoon ground ginger**

Cover tightly and cook slowly for 5 minutes. Toss in

Tomatoes	**1 one lb can bean sprouts**
Peppers	

Bring to a boil, cover and cook briskly for 5 minutes.
Make a paste of

1 tablespoon cornstarch   ¼ cup water

Add to beef mixture and cook until sauce thickens, about 5 minutes. Stir occasionally. When ready to serve, reheat.

Chinese Spareribs

*#1   4 *servings*

In Chinese style . . .
Mash or grind to fine pulp
6 cloves garlic
Mix with
1 tablespoon salt
Mix above ingredients with

1 cup honey   2 cups chicken stock (made
½ cup soy sauce   with 2 bouillon cubes)
                              ½ cup catsup

Marinate overnight in sauce
4 lbs spareribs, cut into small pieces
Baste and turn occasionally. Refrigerate or freeze. When ready to serve, bring to room temperature, put spareribs and marinade in roasting pan and bake at 450° F for 10 minutes, reduce heat and bake at 325° F for 60 to 80 minutes. Baste frequently. Serve with marinade and rice.

Churrasco Roast

#2   8 *to* 10 *servings*

In large shallow roasting pan place
6–8 lb rolled boneless sirloin tip or rump roast
Combine and pour following mixture over roast.

2 tablespoons minced onion   ½ cup olive or salad oil
2 teaspoons thyme   1 cup wine vinegar
1 teaspoon marjoram   3 tablespoons lemon juice
1 bay leaf crushed   1 clove garlic, minced

Stand at room temperature at least 2 hours, turning beef and spooning marinade over occasionally. Then refrigerate at least overnight. Remove meat from marinade and place on spit; outdoors, 15 minutes to the pound for rare; indoors, 15–18 minutes to the pound for rare. Slice thinly. May be served with juices spooned over.

Daube de Boeuf Provençale

#1   *6–8 servings*

Very French.

Daube indicates a style of braising utilizing red or white wine.

Cut into 1½-inch pieces
4 lbs top round beef
Season with

Thyme   **Salt and pepper**
Bay leaf

Marinate for 2 hours in mixture of

1 bottle dry white wine   3 tablespoons olive oil
Drain the beef and place in deep casserole.
Spread the pieces of beef in layers, alternating with

12 fresh diced bacon rinds   4 tomatoes, chopped
8 carrots, sliced   3 cloves garlic, crushed
2 onions, chopped   16 pitted black olives
1 cup mushrooms, chopped

Place, in center of these ingredients, a
"Bouquet garni" (parsley, thyme, bay leaf tied in piece of cheesecloth)
Add
1 orange peel
Pour the marinating liquor over all. Refrigerate if desired.
To serve, cook at 275° F for 5 hours or to desired degree of doneness. Before serving remove "bouquet garni."

Fondue Bourguignonne

This dish really needs a separate chapter. There is an ordered ritual for eating it and prescribed utensils and pots for cooking it. But there are many substitute utensils that work well, too, and do not detract from the fun or intimacy of this type of dinner.

Each guest will need a plate and 2 forks, one with a long shaft. A casserole or chafing dish is filled with salad oil and kept piping hot over an alcohol flame. The group must be small enough to be within easy reach of the oil—not more than 8 people per pot.

A bowl of bite-sized pieces of very tender beef, such as **sirloin or tenderloin (8 oz per person)**, and a variety of sauces are the ingredients.

The guest, using the long handled fork, takes a piece of beef, places it in the boiling oil, where it sizzles delightfully, and cooks it until it is done as much as he desires. He transfers it to his own place, salts and peppers it and then, using the second fork, dips it in one of the sauces offered, such as those below.

*#3   ½ cup

GARLIC BUTTER

Combine and beat with fork

½ cup softened butter	Salt and pepper to taste
3 cloves garlic, minced	

Refrigerate or freeze. Have at room temperature when serving.

*#3   1½ cups

TOMATO STEAK SAUCE

In saucepan combine all ingredients

1 eight-oz can tomato sauce	2 tablespoons brown sugar
⅓ cup bottled steak sauce	2 tablespoons salad oil

Refrigerate or freeze. When ready to serve, bring to boil. Serve hot.

#3   1¼ cups

HORSERADISH SAUCE

Combine

1 cup sour cream	¼ teaspoon salt
3 tablespoons white horse-radish	Dash paprika

Refrigerate until serving time.

Hollandaise, Béarnaise, curry flavored mayonnaise are additional sauces.

Some or all of the following condiments may also be served:

Chutney, slivered almonds, grated coconut, spiced pineapple tidbits, parsley, small white onions, pickled beets, pickle relish, cocktail onions, olives, salted peanuts, and chives.

Gourmet Leg of Lamb

#1   6 servings

Roast

Leg of lamb

at 300 degrees, 30 to 35 minutes to the pound, basting frequently with the following sauce.

Beat well

2 tablespoons chili sauce

1½ tablespoons Worcester-shire sauce

1½ tablespoons vinegar

3 tablespoons olive oil

Dash of each: salt, pepper, thyme, and powdered bay leaf

Stir in

1 ten and a half-oz can beef bouillon

2 tablespoons minced onion

1 clove garlic

Lamb may be wrapped in aluminum foil and reheated when ready to serve.

Ham-and-Tongue Mousse

#2   6 servings

Lovely to look at, delightful to eat.

Sauté for 2 to 3 minutes

3 tablespoons finely chopped shallots

in

1 tablespoon butter

Dissolve

2 envelopes unflavored gelatin

in

⅓ cup dry white wine

Add to dissolved gelatin

2 cups hot chicken stock

Reserve enough clear liquid to cover bottom of 1½-quart mold. Pour into mold and chill until sticky-firm.

Decorate with

Halved, pitted black olives

To remaining gelatin mixture add shallots.

Cube 2⅓ cups cooked smoked ham. Place in blender

½ cup hot liquid   ⅔ cup ham (from 2⅓ cups)

Blend thoroughly. Pour mixture into bowl. Repeat process until all liquid and all ham are blended.

Into ham mixture stir

2 tablespoons brandy   **Salt and freshly ground pep-**
1½ tablespoons tomato   **per to taste**
   paste

Cool mixture. When it starts to thicken add

½ cup finely diced, cooked   **1½ tablespoons fresh dill,**
  tongue   **minced (or 1 teaspoon**
                          dried dill)
                          ¾ cup heavy cream, whipped

Spoon into mold and chill overnight. To serve, unmold on bed of greens and serve with Sour Cream Horseradish Sauce.

SOUR CREAM HORSERADISH SAUCE

#3   *1 cup*

Combine and chill until serving time

1 cup sour cream   **1 teaspoon prepared mustard**
2 tablespoons prepared white
  horseradish

Hamburger Kebob

#1   *6 servings*

Excellent for cookouts.

Combine

1¾ lbs ground chuck   **Salt**
2 teaspoons grated onion   **Pepper**
Dash Worcestershire sauce

Make into walnut-sized balls and broil until brown. Broil
6 strips bacon, cut in half
Sauté

12 mushroom caps   **6 chicken livers, cut in half**
in
2 tablespoons butter
Thread on 6 skewers in this order:

Hamburger   **Folded bacon**
Mushroom cap   **Chicken liver**
End with meat. Dip all in
Melted butter
Broil either outside or inside turning frequently.

Lamb Curry

* # 1   *6–8 servings*
Sauté until golden

2 cloves garlic   **4 onions, sliced**
in
¾ cup butter
Add
3 lbs raw cubed lamb, dredged in flour
Sauté for 10 minutes. Stir. Add

3 tablespoons curry powder   **3 tart apples, peeled and**
                                  chopped
Simmer for 5 minutes. Stir. Add

1 cup walnuts, chopped   **4 tablespoons coconut**
2 lemons, sliced   **4 tablespoons brown sugar**
4 tablespoons raisins   **1 tablespoon salt**
Pour over all
3 cups water
Bring to boil. Reduce heat, simmer for 1 hour. When
ready to serve, reheat.

Indian Pilaf

*#1   *4 servings*

Unusual use of leftover meat.

Bring to a boil

1 cup rice	1 teaspoon curry powder
2½ cups chicken stock	

Cook slowly until liquid is absorbed.
Sauté until golden

4 sliced onions

Add

½ cup white raisins	2 small bay leaves, crushed
4 tablespoons salted almonds, chopped	½ teaspoon nutmeg
½ teaspoon cinnamon	Pepper

Mix with rice. Add

2 cups cooked chicken or lamb

cut in julienne strips. Freeze or refrigerate. When ready to serve, reheat.

Italian Grill

#1   *6 servings*

For cookouts.

Cut into 1½-inch cubes

3 lbs boneless veal

Marinate meat for 2 hours in mixture of

1 cup Italian dressing	1 teaspoon oregano

Scrub, cube, and parboil

1 lb zucchini

Cut into squares

3 red peppers

Cut into cubes

½ lb sharp cheddar

Wrap each cheese cube with

½ slice bacon

Alternately thread ingredients on skewers. Refrigerate. Outdoors or indoors broil 2–3 inches from heat, about 20 minutes.

Lasagna

*#3   6–8 servings

If you like Italian food, don't miss this!
Simmer uncovered

1 one-lb twelve-oz can peeled tomatoes	1½ teaspoons oregano
	⅛ teaspoon pepper
2 eight-oz cans tomato sauce	1 teaspoon onion salt
1 teaspoon salt	

In skillet sauté until light brown

1 cup minced onions	1 clove garlic, minced

in

3 tablespoons olive or salad oil
Add

1 lb ground chuck or round	1 teaspoon salt
1 teaspoon MSG	

Cook until meat is light brown. Add to tomato sauce and simmer 2½ hours or until thickened.

Cook according to package directions
1 one-lb box lasagna noodles
Drain and separate noodles on paper.
For layering:

1 lb ricotta cheese	1 eight-oz package mozzarella cheese, thinly sliced
1 cup Parmesan cheese, grated	

Cover bottom of casserole with several spoonfuls of sauce. Top with criss-cross layer of noodles, then ricotta, mozzarella, and Parmesan. Repeat, ending with sauce and topping with mozzarella. Refrigerate or freeze. When ready to serve, bring to room temperature and bake at 350° F for 50 minutes.

Meat Sauce for Spaghetti

*#3   4 servings

Brown slowly in saucepan

1 lb ground chuck	½ medium onion, chopped
1 tablespoon olive oil	1 teaspoon parsley
1 garlic clove, crushed	

Add

1 one-lb can tomatoes	½ teaspoon basil
2 six-oz cans tomato paste	1 teaspoon oregano
⅛ teaspoon pepper	

Cover pan and simmer 1 hour. Add

1 tablespoon butter

When ready to serve, reheat and serve over

1 lb spaghetti

Pastisto

*#2   6 *servings*

Cook, then drain

1 lb elbow macaroni

Sauté for 3 minutes

2 onions chopped	1 lb ground chuck
in	

¼ lb melted butter

Add

1 tomato peeled and	Salt
chopped	Pepper

Cook until meat is brown and tender. Blend in

½ cup grated American cheese

In buttered casserole place half of macaroni, cover with meat. Top with rest of macaroni. Top with meat. In small saucepan, melt

2 tablespoons butter

Remove from heat and blend in

2 tablespoons flour

Slowly blend in, stirring

1 cup milk

Add

¼ cup grated American	1 beaten egg
cheese	

Return to low heat and cook until thickened.

Pour over macaroni. Refrigerate or freeze. When ready to serve bring to room temperature and bake at 350° F for 40 minutes.

Pot Roast

*#1   *8 servings*

Excellent flavor.

Cut small and fry until golden

6 medium onions

in

2 tablespoons shortening

Set onions aside. In heavy pot brown on all sides

6 lbs brisket of beef

Sprinkle with

Salt   **Pepper**

Cover tightly and simmer slowly for 2½ hours. Then add

Onions   **2 tablespoons brown sugar**
1 cup catsup   **1 ten and a half-oz can to-**
2 tablespoons lemon juice   **mato soup**

If you wish, freeze at this point. When ready to serve, defrost and cook another ½ hour. Reheat at serving time. Excellent with potato pancakes (p. 23).

Rolled Cabbage

*#3   *4–6 servings*

Boil until soft, 15–30 minutes

1 medium head cabbage

Cool and remove leaves carefully. This is best accomplished by first removing core. Combine and mix thoroughly

1 lb ground chuck   **1 medium onion finely**
                                         chopped

Place small amount of meat in leaf (depending on size of leaf) and roll.

In pot place cabbage rolls with

1 sliced onion   **Lemon juice**
1 one-lb can whole tomatoes   **Raisins**
Brown sugar   **Salt or citric acid salt**

(The amount of sugar and lemon varies so greatly depending on individual taste that frequent tasting is necessary and no set proportions can be given.) Simmer, covered, very slowly for 2 hours. Refrigerate or freeze. When ready to serve, return to room temperature, place in shallow pan in oven for ½ hour at 350° F. Baste often and brown well. Adjust seasoning if necessary.

Saltimbocca

*#2   4 servings

An elegant Italian dish.
Start with

8 thin slices prosciutto ham   2 lbs thin veal steak cut in
                                 8 pieces, and flattened to
                                 ⅛ inch

Top each piece of veal in the following order

Slice of mozzarella   Pinch ground sage
Slice of prosciutto   Pinch salt
1 teaspoon melted butter   1 teaspoon snipped parsley
Pinch freshly ground pepper   Second piece of veal

Pinch edges of top and bottom veal slice together. Dip in flour to coat both sides. In large skillet, heat

4 tablespoons butter   4 tablespoons olive oil

Sauté Saltimbocca on both sides, until lightly brown.
Refrigerate or freeze until ready to serve. To serve bring to room temperature, pour on
⅓ cup sherry
Simmer about 20 minutes or until tender. May be served from chafing dish.

Satés

*#1   6 servings

MARINADE

Mash thoroughly and combine

6 grated Brazil nuts   1 tablespoon salt
2 tablespoons coriander   1 hot red pepper, seeded and
  seeds   chopped
2 garlic cloves, minced

Add to above mixture

8 onions grated
2 tablespoons brown sugar
4 tablespoons soy sauce

1 teaspoon ground black pepper
3 tablespoons lemon juice

Marinate overnight in this mixture

2 lbs lean pork cubes

Refrigerate or freeze. When ready to serve bring to room temperature and broil on both sides.

Shish Kebobs

*#1   *6 servings*

Excellent for outdoor cookery, too.

Cut up into 1-inch cubes

½ of leg of lamb (use 3–4 lbs lamb)

Marinate for at least 6 hours in mixture of

6 tablespoons lemon juice
4 tablespoons olive oil
2 tablespoons grated onion
½ teaspoon cayenne

1 teaspoon ginger
1 clove garlic, mashed
2 teaspoons curry powder
1 tablespoon salt

The marinated meat may be frozen or refrigerated.
When ready to serve thread alternately on 6 skewers

Meat
18 mushroom caps
24–30 canned pineapple
  chunks

2 green peppers, cut into
eighths

Broil for 45 minutes.

Spaghetti Superb

*#1   *6 servings*

Lightly brown

1 lb ground chuck
½ cup chopped onion

¼ cup chopped green pepper

in

2 tablespoons shortening

Stir occasionally. Add and heat

1 **ten and a half-oz can cream of mushroom soup**	1 **clove garlic, minced**
1 **ten and a half-oz can to-mato soup**	½ **lb spaghetti, cooked and drained**
1 **soup can water**	½ **cup shredded sharp cheese**

Place in 3 quart casserole. Top with
½ **cup shredded sharp cheese**
Refrigerate or freeze. To serve bake at 350° F for 30 minutes.

Steak Diane

4 servings

For husbands to make in front of the company!
In a large heavy skillet melt
4 **tablespoons butter**
Sauté in it until golden
2 **tablespoons shallots**
Put in skillet
4 **individual portions sirloin steak (about 2 lbs) pounded and trimmed**
Sear them quickly on both sides. Add
2 **tablespoons heated brandy**
Flame the brandy and when it dies down add

4 **tablespoons dry sherry**	**Worcestershire sauce**
Chopped chives	**Steak sauce**
Minced parsley	2 **tablespoons butter**

Mix well. Sprinkle steaks with
Salt and freshly ground pepper
Continued to sauté until done. Because the steaks are so thin they will take very little time to cook.

Stuffed Sweet Peppers

*#1   *6 servings*

Cut in half, lengthwise
3 **large green peppers**

Remove seeds and scald in hot water 4–5 minutes. Drain and fill with following mixture:

In large skillet brown

1 lb ground veal   ½ onion, chopped

in

2 tablespoons butter
 Add

1 cup boiled rice   2 chopped hard-boiled eggs
2 scalded, peeled tomatoes, 2 tablespoons sour cream
 chopped

Season to taste with

Salt and pepper
 Stuff pepper halves and place in baking dish.
 Sprinkle with

Grated American cheese
 Refrigerate or freeze. When ready to serve return to room temperature and bake at 350° F for ½ hour.

Sweet-and-Sour Tongue

*#1   *4 servings*
 Also excellent for using left-over tongue.
 Cook

6 slices bacon
 Remove from pan. Sauté

2 sliced onions in bacon drippings
 Blend in

2–3 tablespoons flour
 Slowly add

4 cups beef stock (made with 4 bouillon cubes and 4 cups of water)
 Let thicken and add

4 tablespoons honey   4 tablespoons vinegar
1 cup raisins   4 cups tongue, julienned

Refrigerate or freeze. When ready to serve, bring to room temperature and simmer for 15 minutes. Garnish with bacon.

Teriyaki

*#1   *6 servings*

Nice outside, too.

Combine

1 tablespoon finely chopped fresh ginger or 2 teaspoons powdered

2 cloves garlic, chopped fine

1 medium onion, chopped fine

2 tablespoons sugar

½ cup soy sauce

1 cup water

Pour this mixture over

2 lbs sirloin steak cut into strips ¼ inch thick

Marinate overnight. Refrigerate or freeze. When ready to serve bring to room temperature, place meat on shallow pan and broil 3–5 minutes on each side.

Veal and Water Chestnuts

*#2   *6 servings*

Brown

2 lbs boneless veal, cut for stew

in

4 tablespoons butter

Add

1 clove garlic, crushed

1 medium onion, grated

Transfer meat to covered casserole. In same frying pan sauté

1 lb fresh mushrooms, sliced

Add mushrooms to meat.

Add to casserole

½ cup beef bouillon

⅛ teaspoon nutmeg

1 bay leaf

1 twelve-oz can water chestnuts, sliced

Stir and cover. Cook at 375° F until tender, about 1½ hours.

Then add

1 cup heavy cream

Cook uncovered for 15 minutes more. Sprinkle with
1 tablespoon parsley
Refrigerate or freeze. When ready to serve bring to room
temperature and reheat.

Veal Parmesan

*#3   6–8 *servings*

SAUCE

Heat in saucepan
¼ cup olive oil
Add and brown lightly

½ cup chopped onion   1 lb ground chuck
Add

2 one-lb twelve-oz cans to-   1 tablespoon salt
matoes (sieved to discard   1 bay leaf
seeds)   1 six-oz can tomato paste
Simmer, covered, 2½–3 hours, until thickened.

VEAL (*#1)

Dip
2 lbs veal cutlets (Italian style—very thin)
into mixture of

Seasoned bread crumbs   Parmesan cheese, grated
then into mixture of

3 eggs, well beaten   Salt and pepper
then into crumbs again. Brown slices on each side in
⅓ cup olive oil
Alternate in casserole layers of

Cutlets   2 eight-oz packages mozza-
Tomato-meat sauce   rella cheese, sliced

Top with sauce. Refrigerate or freeze. When ready to serve
return to room temperature, bake at 350° F for 20 minutes
or until cheese is melted and browned.

Poultry

Baked Imperial Chicken with Cumberland Sauce
*#2   *6–8 servings*

Mix

½ cup grated Parmesan
   cheese

2 cups seasoned bread
   crumbs
3 tablespoons sesame seeds

Cut up into serving pieces
2 two and a half- to three-lb broilers or fryers
   Dip pieces in
½ cup melted butter
then in
Crumb mixture

Freeze or refrigerate. When ready to serve bring to room temperature, place in shallow pan. Dot with

Butter

Bake one hour at 350° F. Serve with Cumberland Sauce if desired.

SAUCE

Combine and simmer until smooth

1 **cup red currant jelly**	4 **tablespoons dry sherry**
1 **six-oz can frozen orange juice concentrate, defrosted**	1 **teaspoon dry mustard**
	⅛ **teaspoon ground ginger**
	¼ **teaspoon hot pepper sauce**

Breezy Barbecued Chicken

*#2   *6 servings*

This took a prize at the Delmarva Chicken Contest!

Marinate in mixture below

2 **two and a half-lb broilers, quartered**

Combine

1 **cup salad oil**	1 **teaspoon dry mustard**
⅓ **cup wine vinegar**	1 **tablespoon Worcestershire sauce**
3 **tablespoons sugar**	
3 **tablespoons catsup**	1 **clove garlic, minced**
1 **tablespoon grated onion**	**Dash hot pepper sauce**
1½ **teaspoons salt**	

Marinate chicken pieces in this sauce overnight. Refrigerate or freeze. To serve, return to room temperature. For outdoors, broil over gray charcoal fire, 12 inches from coals, 20 minutes each side, turning frequently and basting often. If there is any marinade left, serve it hot with chicken. Indoors, broil as far from heat source as possible, basting and turning often.

Chicken and Grapes

#1   *6 servings*

So-o-o elegant but easy!

In large skillet heat

6 **tablespoons butter**

In it brown

2 two and a half-lb fryers, cut into pieces, salted and peppered

Transfer chicken to casserole. In same frying pan brown

2 tablespoons finely chopped onion

Add and heat

1 cup dry white wine

Pour over chickens and bake covered for 30 minutes. Refrigerate.

Bring to room temperature; when ready to serve add

2 cups seedless grapes

Bake the chicken ½ hour more at 350° F.

Chicken Breast Maryland

*#1   *4–6 servings*

*The real name of this lovely dish might scare you away—
Suprêmes de Volaille Virginie—so we translated it, and
since Marian lives in Maryland Virginie changed too.*

Skin and bone (or have your butcher do so)

6 whole chicken breasts

Put each breast between 2 sheets of waxed paper and pound flat with cleaver or rolling pin.

Between the halves of each breast place

1 thin slice well-seasoned ham (shaped to fit breast)

that has been dipped in

4 lightly beaten eggs

Fold over half of breast and press closed at edges. Egg helps to seal it. Dip chicken–ham piece in eggs. Then dip in **Seasoned bread crumbs**

Melt in large skillet

¼ lb plus 2 tablespoons butter

Place chicken breasts in skillet and sauté for 15 minutes, browning on both sides. At this point you may refrigerate or freeze the breasts in a baking dish with the butter sauce poured over them. When ready to serve bring to room temperature and bake for 20 minutes or until heated through at 350° F.

Chicken Breasts Piquant

*#1   *4 servings*

An unusual tang.

Combine

1½ cups rosé or dry red wine
½ cup soy sauce
½ cup salad oil
4 tablespoons water

2 cloves garlic, sliced
2 teaspoons ground ginger
½ teaspoon oregano
2 tablespoons brown sugar

Arrange in baking dish

4 whole chicken breasts

Pour mixture over top. Refrigerate or freeze. When ready
to serve return to room temperature, cover and bake at 375° F
about 1 hour. Serve with rice. (This may also be made with
cut-up whole chicken.)

Chicken Cacciatore

*#2   *4–6 servings*

Cut into individual pieces

2½–3-lb broiler, fryer, or roaster

Sauté pieces until golden brown in

¼ cup or more olive or salad oil

Add

1 large onion, chopped
1 one-lb can whole tomatoes
1 eight-oz can tomato sauce
½ cup dry white wine
1 teaspoon salt

¼ teaspoon pepper
½ bay leaf
⅛ teaspoon thyme
¼ teaspoon marjoram
1 clove garlic, cut up

Cover chicken. Simmer for 1 hour, or until tender.
Refrigerate or freeze. When ready to serve, return to room
temperature, reheat and serve with spaghetti.

Chicken Chinoise

*#1   *6 servings*

Great luncheon casserole.

Cook and then cool in the stock

1 five-pound chicken (or 2 two and a half-lb chickens)

Strain and cool the stock. Cook and drain

½ pound green noodles
Parboil and drain well

4–6 carrots, slivered
Melt

4 tablespoons butter
Stir in

4 tablespoons flour
Add and cook until thick

2 cups chicken stock   **2 tablespoons cream**

Season to taste with

Salt and pepper
Add

Chicken meat, diced   **8 canned water chestnuts,**
Carrots   **sliced**

Line a baking dish with noodles. Pour in chicken mixture. Top with

½ cup prepared packaged stuffing mix
Dot with

Butter

Refrigerate or freeze. When ready to serve bring to room temperature and bake at 400° F for 30 minutes or until hot and bubbling.

Chicken Curry in Pineapple Shells

#1   *6 servings*

Impressive looking and delicious. . . . Not too hot to the taste!

Melt

¼ cup shortening
Add

2 small chopped onions   **1 stalk celery**
1 clove garlic, minced   **1 tart apple, diced**

Cook for 8 minutes, occasionally stirring. Stir in

¼ cup flour   **1 teaspoon salt**
2 teaspoons curry powder   **½ teaspoon dry mustard**

Cook for 2 minutes, stirring. Add
1 bay leaf
Gradually add
2 cups chicken stock
Stir until sauce thickens. Cook for 30 minutes longer over low heat. Add

½ cup light cream
2 tablespoons chutney

1 cup diced fresh pineapple (or crushed canned pineapple, drained, if fresh is not available)

Add
3 cups cooked chicken, diced
Cool.
Cut
3 small pineapples*
in half lengthwise. Cut out fruit, leaving ½-inch thick shell. Two or 3 hours before serving fill shells with mixture.
Top with
Shredded coconut
When ready to serve, arrange on baking dish and bake at 350° F for 20–30 minutes or until heated thoroughly.

Chicken Divan

*#1   6 *servings*
It is divine chicken, too.
Place in bottom of 3 quart casserole
2 ten-oz packages frozen broccoli, cooked
Place on top of broccoli
2 cups of chicken, sliced and cooked
In small saucepan melt
6 tablespoons butter
Blend in
6 tablespoons flour

* If fresh pineapple is not in season, serve filling from casserole over Coconut Rice. See Vegetables, p. 125.

Add gradually, and cook stirring until thick
3 cups chicken stock
Add to sauce

½ cup heavy cream
½ teaspoon Worcestershire sauce
1 cup shredded Parmesan cheese

4 teaspoons prepared mustard
2 tablespoons minced onion
2 tablespoons dry sherry
Salt and pepper to taste

Stir over low heat until cheese is melted. Pour sauce over meat and broccoli. Refrigerate or freeze. When ready to serve, return to room temperature; bake at 400° F for 25–30 minutes. Before bringing to table dash sherry generously over all.

Chicken Florentine

*#1   *6 servings*

Cook according to package directions
2 ten-oz packages frozen chopped spinach
Drain well. Then melt
1 tablespoon butter
Cook in it and stir constantly
1 clove garlic, mashed   **Dash basil**
Dash marjoram
Add and mix well
1 tablespoon flour
Add
⅓ cup medium or heavy cream   **Spinach**

Place mixture on bottom of casserole. Cover with
Meat from 1 five-lb stewed chicken
Melt
3 tablespoons butter
Add and blend well
3 tablespoons flour

Stir in and cook until thickened.

¾ cup cream   Salt and pepper to taste
¾ cup chicken stock

Pour sauce over chicken. Cover with

1 cup grated Parmesan cheese

Refrigerate or freeze. When ready to serve, return to room temperature; bake at 400° F for 20 minutes or until cheese is bubbling.

Chicken Gloriosa

#2   *8 servings*

Over

2 three-lb chickens, cut up

squeeze

2 tablespoons lime or lemon   Salt and pepper
  juice

Let chickens stand for 2 hours.

Drain, reserving juice and sauté chickens in

1 cup oil   2 cloves garlic, crushed

When thoroughly browned, remove chicken to shallow baking dish (9 x 13) and in same oil fry

6 slices very ripe fresh pine-   ½ cup fine bread crumbs
  apple, cut in wedges

Add

Leftover citrus juices   Salt and pepper to taste
1 scant teaspoon hot pepper   ½ cup white raisins
  sauce   4 tablespoons tomato paste
2 pinches saffron   ½ cup sherry

Pour sauce over chicken. Garnish with

1 eleven-oz can mandarin oranges

When ready to serve, cover with foil and bake at 350° F for 1 hour. Serve on

Saffron rice, cooked according to package directions

Chicken in Sour Cream

*#1   *4 servings*

Brown
1 large broiler, quartered
in
3 tablespoons butter
In same pan, brown
1 large onion, chopped
Add

½ cup dry white wine   Pinch basil
2–3 sprigs parsley   Pinch thyme

Sprinkle with **salt and pepper.** Cover and simmer for 1
hour. During last ½ hour add
½ lb whole mushrooms
Refrigerate or freeze. When ready to serve, bring to room
temperature; reheat. Just before serving stir in
½ pint sour cream
Heat but do not boil.

Chicken Italienne

*#1   *6 servings*

Shake
6 breasts of chicken, halved
or
2 broilers, quartered
in bag containing
Flour   Salt

Sauté until golden in
4 tablespoons butter or chicken fat
Place in large casserole.
In same pan used to sauté chicken, brown
4–5 onions, sliced
in
2 tablespoons fat or butter

Add

6–8 stalks celery, cut up
2 three-oz cans broiled mush-
    rooms, sliced

2 ten and a half-oz cans to-
    mato soup
2 six-oz cans tomato paste
1 green pepper, cut up

Simmer ½ hour. Pour over chicken. Refrigerate or freeze. When ready to serve bring to room temperature, cover casserole and bake at 350° F for 1½ hours. Uncover for last 20 minutes. Serve on rice or spaghetti.

Chicken Kiev

*#1   4 servings

Warn your guests about the beautiful spurt of butter when they cut into chicken.

Skin and bone

8 halves of chicken breasts

Be careful not to break the flesh. Place each breast between 2 sheets of waxed paper and pound thin. Do not let flesh split. Cut

5 oz chilled butter

into 8 finger-shaped pieces. Place in middle of each breast, sprinkle with

Salt and pepper   Chives

and roll up breasts, being sure to seal the sides as you roll.
    Dust each roll with

Flour (use about ⅓ cup total)

    Dip in

2 lightly beaten eggs

    Roll in

1⅓ cups bread crumbs

Refrigerate at least 1 hour to make crumbs stick or freeze. To serve, defrost. In electric skillet, heat to 360° F salad oil, enough to fill half way up.

Fry each piece 7 to 10 minutes on each side. Drain thoroughly on absorbent paper and serve.

Chicken Livers and Mushrooms

*#1   *4 servings*

Shake

1 lb chicken livers

in bag containing

Flour   **Salt and pepper**

Sauté in

2 tablespoons butter

Then sauté in same pan

2 sliced onions   ½ lb mushrooms

Meanwhile make sauce of

1 chicken bouillon cube   1 teaspoon sugar
1 cup boiling water   1 tablespoon parsley,
1 tablespoon Worcester-   minced
    shire sauce

Add livers and mushrooms. Refrigerate or freeze. When ready to serve, return to room temperature; reheat slowly and serve on rice.

Chicken Tetrazzini

*#2   *8 servings*

Worth every bit of work.

Simmer until tender, 1¼ to 1½ hours

5 lb roasting chicken

or 45 to 60 minutes

2 two and a half-lb broilers-fryers, cut up

in

4 cups hot water   3 stalks celery
2½ teaspoons salt   1½ teaspoons onion salt
2 onions   1 teaspoon celery seed
4 carrots   1 teaspoon poultry seasoning

Cool. Remove meat in big pieces. Set aside. Also set aside 2 cups stock. Add rest of stock to

Enough water to make 6   3 tablespoons salt
    quarts

When boiling add

1¼ lbs spaghettini

Cook 6 minutes. Drain, place in bottom of large baking dish.

In skillet melt

4 tablespoons butter

Sauté until soft

¾ lb mushrooms, sliced

Sprinkle with

1½ tablespoons lemon juice   ¾ teaspoon salt

Sauté

½ cup sliced almonds

Pour mushrooms and almonds over spaghettini.

Melt, then remove from heat

4 tablespoons butter

Add and blend

2 tablespoons flour   ½ teaspoon pepper
¼ teaspoon paprika   ⅛ teaspoon nutmeg
1½ teaspoons salt

Stir in slowly

¼ cup dry sherry   2 cups chicken broth

Cook and stir until thickened. Remove from heat. Add

1 cup heavy cream

Mix with chicken. Place on top of spaghettini. Refrigerate or freeze. When ready to serve, bring to room temperature, sprinkle with

1 cup Parmesan cheese,   Paprika
grated

Bake at 350° F about ½ to ¾ hour.

Chicken with Almonds

*#1   *4 servings*

Brown

3 lb chicken, cut up

in

6 tablespoons butter

Remove from pan. Add to butter

1 clove garlic, mashed   2 tablespoons onion,
                                  chopped

Remove from heat and stir in until smooth

1 tablespoon tomato paste   2 tablespoons flour

Add and stir until smooth, returning to heat

1½ cups chicken stock

Blend in until at boiling point

2 tablespoons dry sherry

Add browned chicken

2 tablespoons shredded al-   ½ teaspoon tarragon
  monds   Salt and pepper

Refrigerate or freeze. When ready to serve, bring to room
temperature, cover and cook slowly 45–50 minutes. Arrange
chicken in shallow casserole. Stir in

¾ cup sour cream

Pour sauce over chicken. Sprinkle with

1 tablespoon grated cheese

Brown under broiler.

Cold Deviled Chicken

#1   6 *servings*

Split in half or into serving pieces

3 two and a half-lb broilers or fryers

Brush both sides with lots of

Melted butter   Salt and pepper

Place skin side down in broiler for about 20–25 minutes.
Baste often with butter. Turn and broil 10 more minutes.
Put in 400° F oven 10–15 minutes and baste.

Cream together

5 tablespoons dry mustard   4 oz stale beer or water

Spoon generously over chickens. Roll in

1 cup seasoned bread crumbs

Sprinkle with

¼ lb melted butter

Broil 5 minutes until golden. Serve warm or cold.

Deviled Chicken Livers

*#1   4 *servings*

Coat
1 lb chicken livers
with a mixture of
4 tablespoons flour   **1 tablespoon paprika**
Sauté livers and
½ cup chopped onion
in
4 tablespoons butter
Stir in

½ teaspoon salt   **2 teaspoons Worcester-**
Dash pepper   **shire sauce**
Dash cayenne   **1 cup catsup and chili sauce**
1 teaspoon dry mustard   **combined**
                                     1 cup water

Refrigerate or freeze. When ready to serve, return to room
temperature; heat through completely.

Duckling in Wine and Liqueur

#1   4 *to 6 servings*

Wash thoroughly inside and out
2 four and a half- to five-lb ducklings
Dry and rub cavities with
Lemon juice
Put in each cavity
A few celery leaves   **1 onion sliced**

Place ducks, breast side up, on rack in shallow roasting
pan; prick breasts to release fat and roast at 325° F for ½
hour.
Drain fat from pan and add
3 cups white wine
Baste ducks and cook for 1½ hours, basting every 20

minutes. About 15 minutes before finishing, baste ducks with
2 tablespoons honey
Skim off all fat and add to juices remaining

4 tablespoons butter   **2 small cloves garlic,**
Grated rind of 2 oranges   **crushed**
1 cup sliced mushrooms

Bring mixture to boil and simmer gently for 2 minutes.
Remove pan from heat and blend in
6 tablespoons flour
Stir in

½ cup dry sherry   **½ cup Cointreau**
½ cup brandy   **½–⅔ cup orange juice**

Return pan to heat and stir mixture until smooth and
thick. Add

2 tablespoons currant jelly   **2 tablespoons truffle, finely**
                                    chopped (definitely op-
                                    tional!)

Discard garlic and season to taste with
Salt and pepper
Use
Few drops red food coloring
to bring to reddish color. Cut ducks in quarters and refrigerate in sauce until serving time. To serve, reheat ducks in
sauce thoroughly. Arrange ducks on serving platter, mask
with sauce and garnish with
Sautéed whole mushroom   Slices of orange
   caps

Orange Chicken Salad

#1   *4–6 servings*
Combine and chill

4 cups diced cooked chicken   1 cup walnuts, chopped
   meat   **1 cup orange sections**
2 cups thinly sliced celery

DRESSING

Fold together

¼ cup thawed frozen orange juice concentrate

¼ cup mayonnaise

Grated rind of 1 orange

¼ teaspoon hot pepper sauce

1 cup heavy cream, whipped

Toss dressing with salad just before serving.

Serve on

Crisp greens

Paella

#1   *4 servings*

A traditional Spanish delight.

Simmer for two hours

1 five-lb fowl or roasting chicken

Reserve broth. Skin, bone, and dice chicken. In large frying pan place

3 tablespoons olive oil   Diced chicken

Fry until chicken begins to brown, then add

1 large onion, diced   1 clove garlic, crushed

Let onions become transparent, add

2 tomatoes, skinned and mashed

Pinch of saffron (that has been dissolved in 1 teaspoon hot water)

1 cup chicken broth

Simmer 10 minutes. Add

Salt to taste   1 ten-oz package frozen peas

1 cup canned clam juice

Bring to boil. Then add

1 lb raw shrimp, peeled

In another pan heat

1 tablespoon olive oil   1 cup raw rice

Stir until rice is well coated. Add to frying pan.

Stir in

12 medium cherrystone clams (in shells)

Boil 10 minutes. At this point you may refrigerate or freeze. To serve return to room temperature and simmer 15 minutes or until heated through.

Decorate with
Sliced pimiento

Rock Cornish Hen with Cherry-Orange Sauce
#1   *4 servings*

DRESSING

Brown
1 small onion, diced
in
2 tablespoons butter
Add and cook 5 minutes

⅓ cup ham, diced   **⅓ cup mushroom, diced**
Add and mix well
¾ cup cooked wild rice
Use this dressing to stuff
4 individual Rock Cornish hens

SAUCE

Mix together

4 teaspoons cornstarch   **¼ teaspoon dry mustard**
4 tablespoons sugar   **¼ teaspoon ginger**
¼ teaspoon salt
Drain
1 one-lb can red sour, pitted cherries, water packed
Add cherry liquid to cornstarch mixture with

1 tablespoon slivered orange   **¼ cup currant jelly**
rind   **Red food coloring**
½ cup orange juice
Place over medium heat and cook, stirring constantly, until mixture boils and thickens. Add
Drained cherries   **2 tablespoons dry sherry**
When ready to serve, bring to room temperature; bake hens in shallow casserole at 350° F for 45–60 minutes. Baste

often with butter. Just before serving, reheat sauce and serve in sauce dish with hens.

This sauce is also excellent with crisply roasted duckling.

Southwestern Chicken Salad

#1   *4 servings*

Combine

2 cups cooked white chicken   12 small cucumber balls
  meat, in small cubes   Sections from 1 pink grape-
½ cup celery, chopped   fruit
½ cup green pepper,
  skinned, thinly shredded

Add

½ cup French dressing

Toss and chill. Press out excess moisture. Toss again with

½ cup mayonnaise   1 tablespoon parsley, minced
1 tablespoon onion, grated   1 tablespoon chives, minced

When ready to serve, line salad bowl with watercress. Dust salad with

Paprika   Cinnamon
Chopped parsley   Curry

Sprinkle with

2 tablespoons drained capers

Spiced Peaches and Chicken

*#1   *6 servings*

Combine and cook slowly for 10 minutes

1 cup orange juice   2 tablespoons vinegar
1½ cup sliced canned or   1 teaspoon nutmeg
  frozen peaches   1 teaspoon basil
2 tablespoons brown sugar   1 clove garlic, minced

Coat

2 two and a half-lb chickens, cut up
in

½ cup flour   Salt and pepper

Brown chicken on both sides in
Oil to depth of ½ inch in 12-inch frying pan
Pour off oil. Pour sauce over chicken. Refrigerate or freeze.
When ready to serve, bring to room temperature, cover and
simmer 20–30 minutes.

Seafood

Bachelor Crabmeat

3 to 4 servings

1-2-3 done!
Mix together

1 ten and a half-oz can
cream of tomato soup
1 ten and a half-oz can pea
soup
1 cup medium or light cream

¼ cup dry sherry
1 lb crabmeat
½ teaspoon curry powder
¼ teaspoon cayenne

Heat in shallow casserole at 350° F 20–25 minutes. Serve
on toast or rice.

Baked Lobster Savannah

(WITHOUT SHELL)

*#1   4 *servings*

An excellent traditional dish.
Melt in small saucepan
4 tablespoons butter
Add and heat
4 tablespoons flour
Add slowly, stirring until thick
2 cups milk
Add

2 beaten egg yolks   **4 or more tablespoons dry sherry**

Combine with sauce

1 cup fresh mushrooms, chopped   **½ cup green pepper, diced**

Cook over medium heat, stirring constantly, for 15 minutes. Remove from heat and add

2 cups cooked lobster meat   **2 teaspoons paprika**
2 pimientos, sliced   **Salt and pepper to taste**

Pile into casserole. Sprinkle with mixture of

½ cup each   **Grated Parmesan cheese**
Bread crumbs

Refrigerate or freeze. When ready to serve, bring to room temperature and bake at 375° F for 30 minutes.

Cold Poached Salmon with Lemon Sauce

#2   8 *servings*

Excellent summer repast.
Simmer toegther for ½ hour

1 onion   **¼ teaspoon salt**
2 stalks celery   **3-lb piece fresh salmon**
1 cup water

Cool. Meanwhile prepare sauce.

SAUCE

Combine

3 eggs yolks beaten   3½ tablespoons sugar
Juice of 1½ lemons   ½ tablespoon salt

Add

1 cup strained fish broth

Cook until thick. If more gravy is desired

Add

2 teaspoons cornstarch   ½ cup more broth

Serve sauce cold over cold fish.

Crab-and-Mushroom Casserole

*#1   *4 servings*

Sauté for 5 minutes

1 lb sliced mushrooms

in

2 tablespoons butter

Melt

6 tablespoons butter

Blend in

⅓ cup flour

Add and cook until thickened

1 ten-oz can chicken broth   Salt and pepper to taste
1½ cups medium or light
  cream

In 6-cup casserole arrange in alternate layers

Mushrooms   1 lb crabmeat
Sauce

Sprinkle with

Buttered crumbs   Grated American cheese

Refrigerate or freeze. To serve, bring to room temperature
and put casserole in 350° F oven and bake about 30 minutes.

Crabmeat Mandarin

#1   *4 servings*

Cut in half lengthwise

2 small pineapples

Scoop out the inside, leaving ½ inch rim and cut insides into bite-size pieces.

Combine and mix well

1 cup mayonnaise

**1 to 2 teaspoons curry pow-
der**

**3 heaping tablespoons chut-
ney solids, chopped**

2 tablespoons lemon juice

Add and mix well

1 lb crabmeat, flaked

**2 eleven-oz cans mandarin
oranges, drained**

Pineapple

Chill. Liquid will accumulate and should be drained off before placing in pineapple shells, just before serving.

Filet of Flounder with Grapes

#1   *4 servings*

Sauté until tender

½ lb sliced mushrooms

in

3 tablespoons butter

Season with **salt and pepper.**

Poach in large skillet

2 lbs flounder or sole filets

in

1 cup milk

Simmer 5–10 minutes according to thickness of filet. Season with **salt and pepper.** Remove filets carefully.

In saucepan melt

4 tablespoons butter

Remove from fire and add

1½ tablespoons flour

Slowly add milk from poaching. Add

2 tablespoons Parmesan cheese, grated　　　　½ **cup light cream**

Return to fire and stir until it thickens.
Arrange fish, mushrooms, and
½ lb seedless green grapes
in layers in buttered casserole. Cover with sauce and sprinkle with
Parmesan cheese
Refrigerate. When ready to serve, return to room temperature; bake at 400° F for 15 minutes.

Filet of Sole with Crabmeat Sauce

#1　　　　　　　　　　　　　　　　　　　*4 servings*

In saucepan melt
1½ tablespoons butter
Stir in
1 tablespoon flour
Add

½ teaspoon salt	**Pinch onion salt**
½ teaspoon lemon juice	**Dash hot pepper sauce**
¼ teaspoon prepared horse-radish	**⅛ teaspoon MSG**
	Dash pepper
⅛ teaspoon Worcestershire sauce	

Blend in
⅓ cup milk
Cook until thick, stirring constantly. Remove from heat.
Add
1 cup crabmeat
Arrange in greased shallow casserole
2 filets of sole
Pour over them crabmeat mixture. Top with
2 more filets of sole.

Combine and pour over filets

2 tablespoons melted butter

1½ teaspoons lemon juice

Sprinkled with paprika. When ready to serve bake at 350° F for 30 minutes. Serve with lemon wedges.

Hawaiian Shrimp Curry

*#2   6 *servings*

Sauté until golden

2 medium onions, chopped

in

2 tablespoons butter

Make a paste of

7 tablespoons flour	**1½ teaspoon sugar**
1 tablespoon curry powder	**¼ teaspoon powdered ginger**
1½ teaspoon salt	**½ cup chicken bouillon**

Combine this with onion and

2 cups milk   **½ cup chicken bouillon**

Cook over low heat until thick. Meanwhile cook in boiling water for 2 minutes

2 cucumbers, peeled, cut in 2½-inch strips

Drain cucumbers and drop into sauce with

**2 lbs shrimp, cooked and   1 tablespoon onion, minced
cleaned**

When ready to serve, return to room temperature; reheat and serve hot with Coconut Rice (see Vegetables, p. 125).

Lobster Curry

*#1   4 *servings*

In

2 tablespoons butter

Sauté

1 cup onions, chopped	**¼ cup carrots, grated**
½ cup celery, chopped	**1 clove garlic, crushed**
½ cup apples, chopped	

When tender add

2 tablespoons curry powder ¼ teaspoon ginger
1 tablespoon flour 1¼ cups chicken stock
  Simmer for 20 minutes. Put through blender. Add
¼ cup heavy cream 1 ten-oz package frozen peas
2 cups cooked lobtser meat Salt to taste
  Simmer for 5 minutes, until heated through.
  If dish is to be frozen, do not add peas until just before
reheating. Serve with Coconut Rice (see Vegetables, p.
125).

Lobster Macaroni Imperial

*#1   4 *servings*
  Heat together
½ cup butter ½ teaspoon Worcestershire
¼ teaspoon dry mustard sauce
½ 14-oz bottle catsup
  Make layers in casserole of
½ lb elbow macaroni, 1 lb lobster meat
  cooked and drained ½ lb sharp cheddar cheese,
Sauce as above grated
  Refrigerate or freeze. When ready to serve return to room
temperature and place casserole in pan of hot water and
bake at 350° F for 45 minutes.

Margaret's Shrimp Mold

#2   8 *servings*
  Heat
2 ten and a half-oz cans cream of tomato soup
  add
2½ envelopes unflavored gelatin
which has been diluted in
¼ cup cold water

Add

12 ounces cream cheese,
softened
2 cups mayonnaise
1 green pepper, finely
chopped

2 cups celery, finely chopped
1 cucumber, diced
2 teaspoons onion, grated

Place in 6-cup ring mold and jell. To serve, unmold and fill center with

1½ lbs cooked, peeled shrimp

that has been marinated in

French dressing

Top with

Thousand Island dressing

Garnish platter with

Hard cooked eggs
Tomatoes, sliced

Watercress

THOUSAND ISLAND DRESSING (#3)

Combine

1 cup mayonnaise
4 teaspoons chili sauce
1 tablespoon chives
1 teaspoon tarragon vinegar

1 tablespoon green pepper,
chopped
3 tablespoons red pepper,
chopped
1 teaspoon paprika

Refrigerate. Within 4 hours of serving add

½ cup heavy cream, whipped

Piquant Crab Casserole

*#1   *4 servings*

An unusual combination with delightful results.

Cook, according to directions on package

2 ten-oz packages frozen spinach, chopped

Drain well and spread in greased 2-quart casserole. Sprinkle with

1 cup American sharp
cheese, grated

1 pound crabmeat
2 tablespoons lemon juice

Mix and pour over casserole

2 six-oz cans tomato paste	Salt and pepper to taste
1 large onion, minced	Dash of nutmeg
1 pint sour cream	2 tablespoons dry sherry

Sprinkle with

1 cup American sharp cheese, grated

Refrigerate or freeze. When ready to serve bring to room temperature and bake at 350° F about 40 minutes or until bubbly.

Scallop Salad

#1   *4 servings*

In a skillet combine and bring to a boil

½ cup white wine	3 sprigs parsley
¼ cup water	Pinch tarragon
1 onion, peeled	

Add

1½ lbs scallops

Simmer 3–4 minutes for sea scallops, 1½ minutes for bay scallops.

Cool in broth until ready to use. For salad, combine

Scallops, drained	12 sliced green olives
½ lb whole mushroom caps, steamed	Mayonnaise to moisten

Scalloped Oysters

#1   *6 servings*

Mix together

⅔ cup melted butter	3 cups coarse, soda cracker crumbs

Drain, reserving ¼ cup of the liquor

3 dozen shucked oysters

Arrange in a shallow 1½-quart baking dish, alternate layers of crackers and oysters, finishing with top layer of crumbs.

Sprinkle with

2 teaspoons salt	¼ teaspoon pepper

Mix together and pour over top

⅛ teaspoon hot pepper
sauce

¼ cup oyster liquor
½ cup heavy cream

When ready to serve, bring to room temperature; bake at 350° F for 30 minutes.

Scampi

#1   6 servings

Make sauce by combining

½ lb butter, melted
1 teaspoon Dijon mustard
1 teaspoon Worcestershire
sauce
4 cloves garlic, pressed
½ teaspoon chili powder

1 lemon, sliced
Chopped parsley
Salt
Pepper
Paprika
2 tablespoons white wine

Place on jelly roll pan

2 lbs shrimp, cooked with tail shell left on

Pour sauce over shrimp and let stand at least 24 hours in refrigerator. When ready to serve, bake at 350° F for 20 minutes, basting often. Place under broiler for a minute or two until tails turn brown.

Seashore Casserole

*#1   4 to 6 servings

Sauté together

½ lb lobster meat
½ lb cooked shrimp

½ lb crabmeat
1 tablespoon onion, minced

in

¼ cup butter

Melt in small saucepan

3 tablespoons butter

Add and heat

3 tablespoons flour

Add gradually, stirring until thick

1½ cups milk

Fold seafood mixture into this sauce. Then add

2 teaspoons prepared mus-
tard
1 tablespoon Worcester-
shire sauce

1 tablespoon onion, minced
Dash hot pepper sauce
Salt and pepper
2 tablespoons dry sherry

Refrigerate or freeze. When ready to serve, return to room
temperature; heat in top of double boiler and serve over rice,
noodles, or pastry shells or place in casserole, sprinkle with
bread crumbs and cheese. Bake at 400° F 12–15 minutes.

Shrimp-and-Cheese Delight

*#1   4 servings

Sauté for 5 minutes
¼ lb mushrooms, sliced
in
2 tablespoons butter
Lightly mix in

½ lb cooked shrimp
1½ cups cooked rice
1½ cup grated American
cheese
½ cup milk

3 tablespoons catsup
½ teaspoon Worcestershire
sauce
¼ teaspoon salt
⅛ teaspoon pepper

Pour into 2-quart casserole. Refrigerate or freeze. When
ready to bake bring to room temperature and place in 350° F
oven for 25 minutes or until bubbly.

Shrimp-Stuffed Filets

#1   4 servings

Sauté
⅔ cup celery, finely chopped
in
2 tablespoons butter
Combine with

1 lb shrimp, cooked and
chopped

1 large onion, finely chopped

½ cup flavored bread crumbs
1 egg, slightly beaten

Spread on

8 thin flounder or sole filets

Roll up and place in lightly greased baking dish. Pour following sauce over filets. Then top with

Buttered bread crumbs   **Chopped parsley**
**Grated Swiss or Parmesan
cheese**

Refrigerate. When ready to serve bake in 350° F oven 20–30 minutes.

SAUCE

Empty into saucepan

1 package mushroom soup mix

Gradually stir in

2 cups cold water

Heat until boiling.

Add

¼ cup dry white wine

Pour over filets.

Sour Cream Shrimp Curry

#1   *4 servings*

In

2 tablespoons butter

sauté until tender, but not brown

⅓ cup chopped onion   **1 clove garlic, minced**
**¼ cup chopped green pep-
per**

Stir in

1 cup sour cream   **¼ teaspoon salt**
1 teaspoon curry powder   **Pepper**

Add

1¼ lbs shrimp, cooked

Refrigerate. When ready to serve, reheat slowly, stirring and serve with rice.

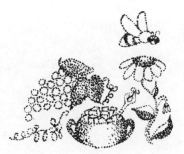

III : Elegant but Easy Accompaniments

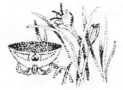

Breads

Barbecued French Bread

*#1   6–8 *servings*

Wonderful with barbecued steak.
Sauté until golden and tender

½ cup chopped onions
in

2 tablespoons butter
Add

1 clove garlic, minced	**2 tablespoons vinegar**
½ cup chili sauce	**2 teaspoons brown sugar**
1 tablespoon Worcester-	**½ teaspoon celery salt**
shire sauce	**1 teaspoon prepared mustard**

Simmer until thickened, about 30 minutes.

Cut in wide slices (don't cut completely through lower crust)

1-lb loaf French Bread

Spread tablespoon of sauce in each cut and sprinkle some of

½ cup grated Parmesan cheese

between cuts and over top of loaf. Wrap in aluminum foil.

Refrigerate or freeze. When ready to serve, bring to room temperature; heat at 400° F for 15 minutes. Unwrap and brown crust. Serve in aluminum foil to keep hot.

Garlic Bread

*#2   *4–6 servings*

Cut in ¾-inch slices, but not quite through to bottom

1 loaf of heat-and-serve French bread

Mix together

¼ lb melted butter	**2 tablespoons chopped pars-**
1 clove garlic, crushed	**ley**

Spread mixture on each slice and over top. Wrap loaf in aluminum foil. Freeze or refrigerate until ready to use. To serve, bring to room temperature and bake at 400° F for 15–20 minutes with foil unwrapped at top until golden brown.

Garlic-Cheese Bread

*#2   *4 servings*

To

4 oz whipped cream cheese

add

¼ cup Parmesan cheese, grated	**½ teaspoon white horse- radish**
1 tablespoon parsley, chopped	**2 teaspoons garlic spread**

Cut 2 small loaves French bread in half lengthwise. Spread mixture over slices. Wrap in aluminum foil. Freeze or refrigerate. To serve, bring to room temperature; bake 15 minutes at 400° F. Cut into large slices.

Herb Bread

*#2

Soften

½ cup butter

Add and mix together

2 tablespoons chopped parsley

1 clove garlic, crushed

¼ teaspoon ground coriander

1 teaspoon ginger

½ teaspoon celery seed

Cut lengthwise and then into 1-inch cross cuts

1 loaf French or Italian bread

Butter all available spaces. Wrap in aluminum foil and freeze or refrigerate until ready to use. To serve, bring to room temperature, then heat in 400° F oven for 10–15 minutes.

Onion Flake Biscuits

A quickie.

Add

2 tablespoons minced instant onion

to

2 tablespoons melted butter

Place

1 package refrigerator biscuits

on baking sheet. Make hollow in center of each with bottom of glass dipped in flour. Fill hollow with onion mixture. Bake at 450° F 8–10 minutes or prepare in advance by baking only 4 minutes. Refrigerate. To serve, bake 4–6 minutes more at same temperature.

Orange, Date, and Nut Bread

*#1

Squeeze the juice from

1 large orange

Add

Boiling water to make 1 cup
Put through food chopper

Orange rind   **½ cup dates**

Place orange mixture in bowl, add orange juice and water. Stir in

1 teaspoon baking soda	**2 tablespoons shortening,**
1 cup sugar	**melted**
	1 teaspoon vanilla

Add

1 beaten egg	**¼ teaspoon salt**
2 cups flour	**½ cup walnuts, chopped**
1 teaspoon baking powder	

Bake in greased loaf pan at 350° F for 1 hour.

Orange Rolls

#3   *12 rolls*

Cream to smooth paste

2 tablespoons soft butter	**Grated rind of 1 orange**
2 teaspoons orange juice	**½ cup confectioners' sugar**

Spread thickly on pan of
Brown and serve rolls, baked

Return to oven for a minute to get them runny and hot.

Popovers

#1   *6 servings*

Into a bowl break

2 eggs
Add

1 cup milk	**½ teaspoon salt**
1 cup sifted flour	

Mix until eggs are blended. Disregard lumps. Pour batter into 6 well-greased five-oz glass custard cups until ¾ full. Set into muffin tins. Place in cold oven. Set oven at 450° F. Turn on heat. Do not open oven for ½ hour. Remove from oven. Puncture 4 sides of neck. Return to oven for 10 minutes with heat off. When ready to serve reheat, placing on cookie sheet so that they do not touch each other. Heat at 350° F for 5 minutes.

Poppy Cheese Bread

*#1
Combine

¼ cup melted butter   ½ cup grated Parmesan
                              cheese

Spread on both sides of
6 one-inch slices of French bread
Sprinkle one side with
1 tablespoon poppy seeds
Refrigerate or freeze. To serve place slices on baking sheet and bake at 350° F for 12 minutes, turning after 6 minutes.

Prune Bread

*#2
Soak for one hour (in water to cover them)
½ lb prunes
Cut them up and pit them. Add

¾ cup boiling water   1 teaspoon baking soda

Let stand for 5 minutes. Then add

¾ cup sugar   ½ teaspoon salt
1 egg   2 tablespoons melted short-
1¾ cup flour   ening

Bake at 325° F for 40 minutes in a greased loaf pan.

Savory Bread

*#1
Cut in thick slices, almost to bottom of crust
1 loaf of French bread
Spread slices with one or more of following spreads:
Cream
½ to ¾ cup soft butter or margarine

with one of the following

Generous pinch each: dried marjoram, thyme, savory

2 tablespoons prepared mustard

½ cup bleu cheese, crumbled

2 cups process sharp cheddar cheese, grated

2 tablespoons chives, snipped

1 teaspoon each: poppy, celery, caraway seeds

Refrigerate or freeze. To serve, bring to room temperature. Bake 15–20 minutes at 375° F.

Vegetables, Greens

Acorn Squash with Applesauce

#1   *4 servings*

Scrub, halve lengthwise, and remove seeds from

2 acorn squash

Mix together

2 teaspoons lemon juice	**¼ cup brown sugar**
¼ cup raisins	**3 tablespoons walnuts,**
1½ cups applesauce	**chopped**

Put mixture into squash halves, dot with

Butter

When ready to serve, place in baking dish with ½ inch hot water in bottom. Cover and bake at 400° F for 1 hour. Remove cover after 30 minutes.

Broccoli and Stuffed Mushroom Caps

#1   *4–5 servings*

Thaw

2 ten-oz packages frozen broccoli spears

Place in 2-quart casserole. Dot with

¼ cup butter   Salt and pepper

Remove and chop the stems from

8 large mushrooms

Sauté caps in

3 tablespoons butter

Remove from pan. In same pan, place stems with

¾ teaspoon onion, minced   ½ teaspoon MSG

Sauté until golden. Fill caps with mixture. Garnish broccoli with caps and

Pimiento strips

Refrigerate. When ready to serve, bake for 45 minutes or until broccoli is tender, at 375° F.

Carrot Cake

#1   *8 servings*

Mix thoroughly in bowl

1 cup shortening   **1¼ cups sifted flour**
½ cup dark brown sugar   **1 cup cooked mashed carrots**
1 teaspoon salt   **(use 2 jars baby food car-**
1 teaspoon lemon juice   **rots)**
1 teaspoon vanilla   **½ teaspoon baking powder**
2 beaten egg yolks   **½ teaspoon baking soda**

Fold in

2 egg whites, stiffly beaten

Bake in greased 2-quart mold at 350° F for 40 minutes. If you wish to finish baking later, refrigerate. When ready to serve, bring to room temperature and bake 20 minutes at 350° F. Unmold. Center may be filled with vegetables.

Cauliflower with Shrimp   Sauce

#1   *6 servings*

Cook 10–15 minutes

1 medium head cauliflower broken into flowerettes

or

2 ten-oz packages frozen cauliflower, according to directions

Mix and season

1 ten and a quarter-oz can   ½ cup sour cream
defrosted frozen cream of
shrimp soup

When ready to serve, heat sauce and cauliflower together.
Add

¼ cup slivered, blanched toasted almonds

Corn in Sour Cream

#1   *8 servings*

Cook until soft

2 tablespoons chopped onion

in

2 tablespoons butter

Add gradually, stirring

½ pint sour cream

Add

2 twelve-oz cans whole ker-   ½ lb bacon, cooked, drained,
nel corn, drained   and crumbled

Refrigerate. When ready to serve, heat through and garnish with parsley.

Eggplant Neapolitan

#1   *6 servings*

Simmer for 30 minutes

2 tablespoons tomato paste   2 tablespoons olive oil
1 one-lb twelve-oz can to-   Salt
matoes

Peel and slice
1 medium-sized eggplant
Dip slices in
Flour   **Salt and pepper**
then in
Beaten egg
Fry for 3 minutes on each side in
Olive oil
Drain. Mix together

2 cups cottage cheese   **1 teaspoon garlic salt**
2 tablespoons parsley,   **½ cup bread crumbs**
chopped

Alternate layers in casserole

Eggplant   **Tomato sauce**
Cheese mixture

Top with tomato sauce. Sprinkle with
Parmesan cheese, grated
When ready to serve, bake at 350° F for 30 minutes.

Eggplant Parmigiana

#1   *6 servings*

Simmer uncovered for 30 minutes

1 one-lb can tomatoes   **2 tablespoons tomato paste**
2 tablespoons olive oil   **Pinch salt**

Wash, dry, and cut into ½-inch slices
1 large eggplant, peeled
Fry for 3 minutes on each side in
Hot olive oil
Mix together

1 cup bread crumbs   **1 clove garlic, crushed**
½ cup Parmesan cheese,   **Salt and pepper to taste**
grated
1 tablespoon parsley,
chopped

Put layer of eggplant on bottom of casserole. Sprinkle with crumbs and pour tomato sauce over all. Alternate layers. Finish with eggplant. Cover with
1 eight-oz package mozzarella cheese, sliced
When ready to serve, bake at 375° F for 20–30 minutes.

Green and Gold Squash

#1   *4–6 servings*
Scrub well and remove stems from
¾ lb zucchini   ¾ lb yellow summer squash
Shred coarsely.
In large frying pan sauté
1 medium onion, chopped
in
2 tablespoons salad oil
Remove from heat. Stir in shredded squash, add
2 tablespoons parsley,   ¼ teaspoon pepper
chopped   3 eggs, slightly beaten
½ teaspoon salt   ½ cup milk
½ teaspoon oregano
Spoon half the mixture into a buttered 1½-quart casserole. Sprinkle with ½ of
1 cup sharp cheddar cheese,   ½ cup saltine crumbs (18
shredded   crackers)
Make a second layer of squash, cheese, and cracker crumbs with remaining ingredients. When ready to serve, bake at 350° F for 45 minutes.

Lima Bake

#1   *6 servings*
Slightly defrost
2 ten-oz packages frozen limas
Place in buttered baking dish and pour following ingredients over. Combine

½ teaspoon salt
¼ cup melted butter
¼ cup milk
2 tablespoons molasses

2 teaspoons prepared mustard
¾ cup sour cream
1 teaspoon Worcestershire sauce

When ready to serve bake for 45 minutes at 350° F.

Mattar-Paneer
(Peas and Cheese)

#1   4 servings

Sauté until soft
1 small onion, sliced
in
2 tablespoons butter
Add

1 ten-oz package frozen peas
1 teaspoon salt
¾ teaspoon turmeric

¾ teaspoon curry powder
2 small mint leaves, minced

Cover and cook until peas are just tender, 5 minutes. Remove from heat and blend in

8 oz creamed large curd cottage cheese

¼ teaspoon chili powder

Refrigerate. When ready to serve, reheat thoroughly over low heat.

Orange-Mint Peas

#1   10 servings

Remove rind from
½ orange
in ½ inch strips, leaving no white on rind. Cut the strips crosswise into very fine slivers to make 3 tablespoons. Heat and steep for a few minutes in
½ cup butter
Add
¼ cup mint, finely chopped

When ready to serve, cook according to package directions
3 ten-oz packages frozen peas
Drain. Add butter mixture and heat thoroughly.

Oven-Crisped Eggplant

#1   *6 servings*

Crush into fine crumbs
½ cup saltines (10 doubles)
Mix the crumbs with

¼ teaspoon oregano   ½ teaspoon salt
½ teaspoon paprika

Peel and cut lengthwise into 6 or 8 segments each
2 small eggplants
Dip pieces in

1 egg mixed with   1 teaspoon water

Then dip in crumb mixture. Let stand at least 30 minutes.
Place peeled side down in shallow pan. Drizzle with
¼ cup melted butter
When ready to serve bake at 400° F for 20 minutes.

Peanut-Topped Squash

#1   *6 servings*

Slice
2½ lbs summer squash
Cook 20 minutes with

3 sliced onions   Salt and pepper to taste
½ cup water

Drain off liquid. Mash.
Chop
¼ lb salted peanuts
Mix with
8–10 coarsely crumbled round salted crackers 2 inches diameter
Season with
Salt and pepper

Add
1–2 tablespoons butter
Place squash in greased baking dish. Top with nuts, dot with butter. When ready to serve bake at 350° F for 30 minutes.

Peas and Black Olives

#1   *6 servings*

Melt
2 tablespoons butter
Add

1 tablespoon minced dried onions	**3 tablespoons chopped pimiento**
¼ teaspoon oregano	**¼ cup chopped ripe olives**
Dash pepper	

Refrigerate. When ready to serve cook
1 one-lb package frozen peas
Drain and add to reheated mixture.

Peas and Water Chestnuts

#1   *6 servings*

Drain and dice
1 five-oz can water chestnuts
When ready to serve, cook according to package directions
2 ten-oz packages frozen peas
Drain. Add

3–4 tablespoons butter	**Salt and pepper to taste**
Water chestnuts	

Heat briefly.

Peas Oriental

*#2   6 *servings*

Mix together in casserole

2 ten-oz packages frozen peas, barely cooked and drained

1 five-oz can water chestnuts, drained and sliced

1 one-lb can bean sprouts, drained

½ lb mushrooms, sautéed in butter

1 ten and a half-oz can cream of mushroom soup

Bake at 350° F for ½ hour. Refrigerate or freeze. When ready to serve bring to room temperature, top with

1 three and a half-oz can French-fried onion rings

Bake 15 minutes more.

Pickled Cucumbers

#7   makes 2 *quarts*

Combine in saucepan and boil for 5 minutes

1 pint white vinegar

1 clove garlic

1 tablespoon whole cloves

1 tablespoon whole allspice

1 bay leaf

1 stick cinnamon

1 tablespoon each: celery seed, whole mustard seed, peppercorns

1 piece dried gingeroot

2 cups sugar

Cool. Then pour marinade over

5 cucumbers, unpeeled, sliced thin

Refrigerate. Stir once a day. Do not serve for at least 4 days. They will keep for weeks.

Salami-Stuffed Tomatoes

#1   6 *servings*

Cut the tops off and remove the pulp from

6 medium tomatoes

Chop

6 anchovy fillets   6 slices salami

Mix with

1 cup bread crumbs   Pinch of basil
1 tablespoon olive oil

Sprinkle tomato cavities with

Salt and pepper

Then stuff with salami mixture. Top with buttered crumbs. When ready to serve, bake at 350° F for 25 minutes.

Sesame Squash

#1   *6–8 servings*

Stem, wash and slice thin

2½ lbs summer squash

Place it in a large frying pan. Add

1 clove garlic, mashed   ¼ cup water

Cover and place over low heat until tender. In separate pan toss

2 tablespoons sesame seeds
in
1 tablespoon butter

Shake over low heat like popcorn until brown. Set aside. When squash is cooked, drain and mash thoroughly.

Add

Salt to taste   **Sesame seeds**

When ready to serve add

⅔ cups sharp cheddar cheese, shredded

Stir well and place over heat, covered, until cheese melts and blends.

Spicy Limas

#1   *6 servings*

In pot combine

2 ten-oz packages frozen   ½ teaspoon pepper
   baby limas   2 tablespoons butter
6 small bay leaves   2 teaspoons salt
2 teaspoons onions, minced   ½ cup water

Cover, bring to boil, reduce heat and cook 15 minutes. Remove bay leaves. Refrigerate. When ready to serve reheat.

Spinach Mornay

*#2   8–10 *servings*

Cook slowly without any additional water
3 ten-oz packages frozen chopped spinach
Drain thoroughly. Season with
Salt and pepper
Melt
4 tablespoons butter
Off heat add
3 tablespoons flour
Season with

Salt	**1½ teaspoon Dijon mustard**
Cayenne pepper	**1 teaspoon dry mustard**

Blend in
1 cup milk
Stir over heat until it boils and add

3 tablespoons Swiss cheese, grated	**¼ cup Parmesan cheese, grated**
	4 tablespoons light cream

Simmer 5 minutes. Combine with spinach and refrigerate
or freeze. To serve, bring to room temperature; heat thoroughly at 350° F about 15 or 20 minutes. Five minutes before removing sprinkle generously with
Parmesan cheese, grated
Also delicious and very attractive if baked in tomato cases,
but tomatoes, remember, are not freezable.

Spinach Tart

*#2   8–10 *servings*

Cook, then drain thoroughly
3 ten-oz packages frozen chopped spinach
Sauté until transparent
1 small minced onion
in
2 tablespoons butter

Mix

3 egg yolks	¾ cup light cream

Season with

Salt and pepper	3 tablespoons grated Par-
Pinch of nutmeg	mesan cheese

Mix all together. Refrigerate or freeze. When ready to serve, bring to room temperature; place in 10-inch pie plate or 2-quart casserole and bake at 350° F for 15 minutes.

String Beans Provençal

#1   *6 servings*

Heat in frying pan

3 tablespoons olive oil

Add and heat

¼ cup capers	1 garlic clove, crushed
¼ cup anchovy fillets	

Cook according to directions

2 nine-oz packages frozen French-style string beans

Season with

Salt and pepper

Add to above mixture. When ready to serve, toss all ingredients until well mixed. Reheat and sprinkle with

1 tablespoon onion, finely chopped

Summer Squash Pudding

#1   *6 servings*

Boil, drain, and mash

4 large summer squash

Add

2 beaten eggs	2 tablespoons sour cream
1 tablespoon sugar	Salt and pepper to taste
1 tablespoon butter	

Place in casserole. Spread top with

Buttered bread crumbs

When ready to serve bake at 350° F for 20 minutes.

Sweet-and-Sour Green Beans

#1   *8 servings*

Cook until crisp

½ lb bacon

Drain, reserve ¼ cup drippings. Crumble bacon.

Beat together

2 eggs	**3 tablespoons sugar**
⅓ cup vinegar	**¼ teaspoon salt**
½ cup water	

Return drippings to skillet. Add egg mixture. Cook stirring constantly until thick. Combine dressing with

1½ lbs green beans, cooked	**Bacon**
and drained	**1 tablespoon diced pimiento**

Refrigerate. When ready to serve reheat.

Tangy Mushrooms

#1   *4 servings*

In

4 tablespoons butter

sauté until tender

1 lb sliced mushrooms	**2 teaspoons onion, grated**

Mix together

2 cups sour cream	**1 teaspoon salt**
4 teaspoons flour	**¼ teaspoon pepper**

Add to mushrooms. Refrigerate. When ready to serve, cook until thickened over very low heat. Stir.

Tomato-Cheese Zucchini

#1   *4–6 servings*

Cut in half lengthwise

3 medium zucchini squash

In

1 tablespoon oil

brown in a 10-inch frying pan

1 medium onion, thinly sliced

Add

Zucchini, cut side up   **Salt and pepper**
1 teaspoon oregano
Pour in
1 eight-oz can tomato sauce
Cover and cook until barely tender, 8–10 minutes. When ready to serve, top zucchini with
1 eight-oz package Mozzarella cheese, sliced
Heat until cheese is melted. Sprinkle with
Parmesan cheese, grated

Tomato Pudding

#1   *6 servings*

Heat for 5 minutes

2 cups canned tomatoes   **Salt and pepper**
Meanwhile butter a 2-quart casserole. Fill with loosely torn pieces of fresh white bread, crusts removed.
Pour over bread
¼ lb melted butter   **Hot tomato liquid**
1 cup light brown sugar
When ready to serve, cover casserole and bake at 350° F for 30 minutes. If mixture looks dry add
Tomato juice

Zucchini à l'Orange

#1   *4 servings*

Sauté in a 10-inch frying pan until just tender
2 lbs zucchini, cut into thin rounds
in
⅓ cup butter
Season with
¾ teaspoon salt   **¼ teaspoon pepper**
Remove from heat and add
3 tablespoons frozen orange juice, undiluted
Refrigerate. When ready to serve simmer until steaming.

Vegetables, Starches

Almond Poppy Seed Noodles

*#1   *8–10 servings*

Melt

½ cup butter

Add and sauté until golden

1½ cups slivered blanched almonds

Stir in

½ cup poppy seeds   **2 eight-oz packages wide egg**
¾–1 teaspoon salt   **noodles, cooked and**
                                              drained

Refrigerate or freeze. When ready to serve, bring to room temperature; reheat in top of double boiler.

Baked Stuffed Potatoes

#2   6 *servings*

Cut in half lengthwise and scoop out pulp from
6 large Idaho potatoes, baked
Mash pulp slightly and place in mixer.
Add

4 egg yolks   **¾ cup butter**
4 tablespoons light cream   **Salt and pepper to taste**

Whip until smooth and light.
Fold in
4 stiffly beaten egg whites
Put back in shells. Sprinkle lightly with
Buttered bread crumbs

If you wish to refrigerate for a day or two before serving,
bake the potatoes at 350° F for 10 minutes to set the egg
whites. When ready to serve, bake the potatoes for 20 minutes at the same temperature until hot and browned.

Baked Sweet Potatoes with Orange Glaze

#1   6 *servings*

Combine

⅓ cup brown sugar   **1 tablespoon cornstarch**
⅓ cup granulated sugar

Add

1 cup orange juice   **Pinch salt**
**2 teaspoons grated orange
rind**

Pour sauce over

6 cooked or canned sweet   **1 orange, thinly sliced with
potatoes, sliced horizon-   rind**
tally**

When ready to serve bake in covered casserole for ½ hour
at 350° F. Remove cover and bake ½ hour more.

Brown Rice Oriental

*#1   *4 servings*

In
¼ cup butter
brown until golden, stirring often
1 cup raw brown rice
    Dissolve
3 chicken bouillon cubes
in
2 cups hot water
    Combine with

½ cup green pepper, chopped	2 tablespoons minced onion
	¼ cup pimientos, diced
Browned rice	1 tablespoon soy sauce

Turn into 1½-quart casserole. Refrigerate or freeze. When ready to serve, bring to room temperature and bake at 350° F for 45 minutes, covered. Uncover and add
1 five-oz can water chestnuts, sliced
    Bake 10 minutes longer.

Coconut Rice

#1   *4 servings*

Bring to a boil

2½ cups water	1 teaspoon salt

Stir in
1 cup raw rice
    Cook, covered until water is absorbed, about 25 minutes. Then add

⅓ cup toasted coconut	Salt and pepper to taste
2 tablespoons butter	

Reheat in top of double boiler.

Cornflaked Potatoes

#2   *6 servings*

Impressive looking.

Wash, pare, and boil until tender
6 medium-sized potatoes
in
4 cups boiling, salted water
Drain and mash well, adding

3 tablespoons butter	**Dash onion salt**
1 teaspoon salt	**Dash pepper**
⅓ cup hot milk or cream	

Roll potatoes into six balls.
Dilute
1 beaten egg
with
2 tablespoons water
Roll potato balls in egg, then in
Crushed cornflakes

When ready to bake, place on greased baking sheet and
bake at 375° F until well heated—about 20 minutes.

Fruited Rice

#1   *4 servings*

Place in 1½-quart greased casserole
1 cup quick cooking rice
Combine and pour over

½ cup finely chopped celery	**1 three-oz can crushed pine-**
1 one-lb package frozen rhu-	**apple, drained**
barb, defrosted	**⅓ cup water**
	1 teaspoon salt

Refrigerate. When ready to serve bake at 300° F for 1
hour.

Gnocchi

*#2   6 *servings*

Bring to a boil
1 quart milk
Add to it
¼ cup butter, cut into pieces
Gradually stir in
1 cup regular hominy grits
Resume boiling and continue to cook and stir about 5 minutes. Remove from heat and add

1 teaspoon salt   **⅛ teaspoon pepper**

Beat hard with electric mixer for 5 minutes. Pour into 9x13 pan. Allow to set. Then cut into rectangles. Place them one over the other like fallen dominoes, in a buttered shallow casserole. Over them pour
⅓ cup melted butter
Sprinkle with

1 cup Swiss cheese, grated   **⅓ cup Parmesan cheese, grated**

Refrigerate or freeze. To serve, bring to room temperature; heat through in a 400° F oven for 30–35 minutes.

Italian Potato Soufflé

*#1   9 *servings*

Combine

3 tablespoons Parmesan cheese   **9 boiled, mashed potatoes**
                                      3 eggs beaten

Alternate layers in casserole of

Potatoes   **1 eight-oz package mozzarella cheese, sliced**

Top with

Buttered crumbs   **Parsley**

Refrigerate or freeze. When ready to serve, bring to room temperature; bake at 375° F for 45 minutes.

Lemon-Glazed Sweet Potatoes

*#1   *8 servings*

Dice into buttered casserole
8 cooked sweet potatoes
Make a syrup of

¾ cup water	**ade concentrate**
½ cup sugar	**(undiluted)**
4 tablespoons frozen lemon-	**4 tablespoons butter**

Boil for 5 minutes. Pour over potatoes. Decorate with
½ cup miniature marshmallows

Refrigerate or freeze. When ready to serve, bring to room
temperature; bake at 400° F for 30 minutes or until heated
through.

Marian's Noodle Pudding

*#1 ·   *12 servings*

Even Lois admits this one is great!
Cook according to package directions
1 lb broad egg noodles
Drain and rinse with cold water. Mix noodles with

1 pint sour cream	**2½ teaspoons salt**
1 lb cottage cheese	**4 tablespoons sugar**
1 cup milk	**6 tablespoons melted butter**

Place in shallow greased casserole; top with
Crushed cornflakes
dot with
Lots of butter

Refrigerate or freeze. When ready to serve, bring to room
temperature; bake at 375° F for 1½ hours.

Potatoes Parmesan

#1   *4–6 servings*

Peel, dice, and pat dry
2 lbs potatoes
Place in large frying pan with

3 tablespoons butter	**3 tablespoons cooking oil**

Cover and cook until tender (about 15 minutes) stirring often.

Add

1 tablespoon beef bouillon   3 tablespoons Parmesan
                                 cheese, grated

Transfer to casserole and sprinkle top with

3 more tablespoons cheese   Paprika

When ready to serve, bake uncovered at 350° F for 30 minutes.

Rice-and-Mushroom Ring

*#1   *6 servings*

Cook according to directions (see Coconut Rice, p. 125)

1 cup raw rice

Rinse in warm water. Put through medium grinder

1 lb raw mushrooms

Sauté mushrooms in

2 tablespoons butter

Add rice and

Salt to taste

Simmer 15 minutes. Put in buttered 2-quart mold. Refrigerate or freeze. When ready to serve, bring to room temperature; set in pan of boiling water and bake at 350° F for 45 minutes. Serve with peas in center if desired.

Sweet Potatoes Charleston

#2   *6 servings*

Mix together in large casserole

2 cups sweet potatoes,   1 orange, sliced
  cooked and sliced   2 tablespoons lemon juice
½ cup brown sugar   ⅓ cup water
1 tablespoon flour   3 tablespoons butter
1½ teaspoons salt

When ready to serve, bake in covered casserole for 35 minutes at 350° F. Remove cover to brown for 10 minutes more.

Tibetan Rice

*#1   *4 servings*

Place in saucepan

1 cup raw rice   2 tablespoons salad oil

Cook over direct heat, stirring until rice is well coated. Blend in

¾ teaspoon turmeric   ¾ teaspoon salt
¾ teaspoon curry powder   ½ cup raisins

Combine

1½ cups boiling water   2 chicken bouillon cubes

Stir into rice mixture. Refrigerate or freeze. When ready to serve, bring to room temperature; cover and cook over simmering water 1 hour or until rice is fluffy and liquid absorbed.

Tisket-A-Tasket Sweet Potatoes

#2   *10 servings*

SWEET POTATO FILLING

Combine thoroughly

3 cups mashed cooked sweet   Molasses to taste
  potatoes   ½ teaspoon cinnamon
2 tablespoons soft butter   ¼ teaspoon cloves
½ teaspoon salt   ¼ teaspoon ginger
½ teaspoon grated lemon   ½–¾ cup crushed pine-
  rind   apple, drained
2 well-beaten eggs

Cut 5 large oranges in half and scoop out the pulp. Fill with sweet potato mixture. Bake at 350° F 20 to 25 minutes.

Turkish Rice

                                            4 servings

A quickie, and so much more delicious than regular rice!
Melt

⅛ lb butter

Add

½ cup raw rice
Stir until golden. Add

1 can beef bouillon
Cover pan. Simmer until liquid is gone, about 20 minutes.

Vegetable Fried Rice

*#1   8–10 *servings*
Cook according to directions (see Coconut Rice, p. 125)

1 cup raw rice
Chop together

8 mushrooms	3 pimientos
8 water chestnuts	1 large onion

Drain

1 five-oz can bamboo shoots
Beat together

2 eggs	1 teaspoon cornstarch
¼ cup water	2 teaspoons peanut oil

Put enough peanut oil in bottom of skillet to cover. Scramble eggs over low heat for 1 minute. Turn heat high, add rice and vegetables and season with

3 tablespoons soy sauce   ½ teaspoon MSG
Stir and fry for 6 minutes. When ready to serve, reheat.

Wild Rice Party Dish

*#2   6 *servings*
In heavy frying pan place following ingredients:

¼ lb butter	½ lb sliced mushrooms
1 cup wild rice, prepared*	1 teaspoon salt
½ cup slivered almonds	2 tablespoons sherry
2 tablespoons onion, chopped	

* To prepare wild rice: Wash quickly in cold water. Pour boiling water over it to cover and let stand ½ hour; drain. Repeat and let stand until water cools, drain. Proceed as directed in recipe.

Cook until rice is well coated, stirring frequently. Place in casserole with

3 cups chicken broth

Cover. Refrigerate or freeze. When ready to serve, return to room temperature, then bake covered at 325° F for 1 hour and 15 minutes, until liquid is absorbed.

Salads

Armenian Vegetable Salad

#2   *8 servings*

Mix together

2 nine-oz packages frozen
cut beans, slightly under-
cooked

1 seven-oz can pitted black
olives, drained and sliced

1 four-oz can pimiento,
drained and sliced

1 bunch scallions, white part
only, sliced

1 eight-oz can button mushrooms, drained

Marinate overnight in
Well-flavored French dressing

Serve without lettuce in large glass bowl for this is beautiful as well as delicious. Let stand at room temperature for
15 minutes before serving.

Avocado Aspic

#1   *4 servings*

Tart and tangy!

Dissolve

1 three-oz package raspberry gelatin

with

2 cups hot tomato juice

Add and mix

1 tablespoon prepared horseradish

Pour in bottom of 1-pint mold a small amount of gelatin mixture and chill until sticky firm. On this place

Slices of small avocado

Cover with remaining gelatin and refrigerate to jell. Unmold.

Blueberry-Lemon Mold

#2   *8–10 servings*

Dissolve

1 three-oz package lemon gelatin

in

1 cup boiling water

Cool. Add and stir until smooth

½ pint sour cream

Pour into 2-quart mold. Jell. Dissolve

3 three-oz packages raspberry gelatin

in

3 cups boiling water

Drain, reserving syrup

2 fifteen-oz cans blueberries

Add to raspberry gelatin

2 cups blueberry syrup

Cool, add

Drained blueberries

Pour over jelled sour cream mixture. Jell. Unmold.

Caraway Fruit Ring

#1   *8–10 servings*

Drain, reserving syrup

1 one-lb-14-oz can fruit cocktail

Combine

Syrup   **2 teaspoons caraway seeds**
1¾ cups water   **¼ teaspoon salt**

Boil 3–5 minutes. Pour hot syrup over

2 three-oz packages lemon gelatin

Blend in

½ cup lemon juice

Chill until consistency of unbeaten egg whites.
Fold ½ gelatin mixture into

Fruit cocktail

Turn into 2-quart mold. Into remaining gelatin fold in

½ pint sour cream   **2 cups cheddar cheese,
                                      shredded**

Pour on top of first layer when it is firm. Chill. Unmold
to serve.

Cherry-Polka Dot Mold

#2   *8 servings*

Colorful and delicious!

Dissolve

2 three-oz packages cherry gelatin

in

2 cups hot water

Add

3 tablespoons lemon juice   1¾ cups cold water

Pour enough of mixture into 6½-cup mold to cover bottom. Chill until partially set.

Shape into about 30 small balls

8 oz cream cheese

Alternate in bottom of mold with

Portion of 1½ cups cantaloupe balls

and/or

Honeydew balls

Place enough of

⅔ cup pecan halves

around outer edge of mold to make ring. Chill until firm. Meanwhile chill remaining gelatin until partially set. Add to it remaining

Cheese and melon balls, pe-   **½ cup sliced stuffed green**
can halves and   **olives**

Pour over first mixture and jell in refrigerator. Unmold.

Coconut-Orange Mold

#2   *8 servings*

Dissolve

2 three-oz packages orange gelatin

in

1½ cups hot water

Add

2¼ cups juice, orange and canned pineapple*

Chill until slightly thick. Add

1 one-lb four-oz can crushed   **½ three and a half-oz pack-**
pineapple, drained   **age coconut**
½ pint sour cream

Place in 2-quart mold. Jell in refrigerator. Unmold.

Fourth of July Mold

#3   *16 servings*

Stupendous red, white, and blue creation!

Line bottom of 12-cup oiled mold with

1 one-lb three-oz can peach halves, drained

Place cut side down with

Maraschino cherries

under center of each half.

* Always use canned pineapple—never fresh or frozen—for gelatin molds or the mold will not jell!

Prepare

1 three-oz package raspberry gelatin
with

¾ cup boiling water   ¾ cup peach syrup

Chill until slightly thick. Pour over peaches. Refrigerate until firm.

Blend until smooth

**1 cup sour cream   1 eight-oz package cream
                              cheese, softened**

Prepare

2 three-oz packages pineapple gelatin
with

1½ cups boiling water   1½ cups pineapple juice

Chill until slightly thick. Add to cream mixture

1 cup drained crushed pineapple (one-lb four-oz can)

Add cream mixture to slightly thickened gelatin. Then pour on top of jelled mixture. Prepare

1 three-oz package black raspberry gelatin
with

¾ cup boiling water   ¾ cup blueberry syrup

Chill until slightly thick. Fold in

1 fifteen-oz can drained blueberries

Pour into mold; jell in refrigerator. Unmold to serve.

Fruited Apricot Mold

#2   6 *servings*

In saucepan combine

**1 three-oz package orange   ¾ cup water
   gelatin   1 twelve-oz can apricot nec-
1 envelope unflavored gelatin   tar
2 tablespoons sugar**

Over low heat, stir until gelatins dissolve. Add

2 tablespoons lemon juice

Pour enough of mixture into 2-quart ring mold to cover

bottom and chill until sticky firm. When barely firm arrange
on bottom of mold

3 oranges, sectioned and   1 one-lb one-oz can spiced
  seeded   grapes, drained

Pour on ½ of remaining apricot mixture. Refrigerate until
almost jelled. Meanwhile combine remaining apricot mixture
with

1 eight-oz package cream   1 one-lb four-oz can pine-
  cheese, softened   apple chunks, drained

Pour on top of jelled mixture. Refrigerate. When ready to
serve, unmold.

Gorgonzola Salad

#1   6 servings

Combine, cover well, and refrigerate

1 head of lettuce, chopped   1 medium onion, chopped
1 green pepper, diced   fine
                                ¼ cup celery, diced

Combine and refrigerate

6 tablespoons olive oil   Salt and pepper
6 tablespoons cider vinegar

When ready to serve, place greens in garlic-rubbed bowl.
Toss with oil and vinegar.
Add
2 quartered tomatoes
Top with
½ cup or more Gorgonzola cheese, shredded

Green-Bean Salad

#1   4 servings

Prepare according to directions
1 nine-oz package frozen French-style string beans
Cool. Then marinate for 24 hours in
French dressing

When ready to serve place on bed of
Lettuce leaves
Decorate with
Cucumber slices
Top with
Dollop of sour cream   Dash paprika

Macédoine Salad

#1   *8 servings*
Cook until just tender
1 ten-oz package frozen peas
Chill immediately with ice cubes to stop further cooking.
Drain. Combine peas with
1 medium cucumber, sliced   **2 tablespoons chives, minced**
thin
Marinate at least 1 hour or as long as overnight in
1½ cups French dressing
Peel and dice
1 avocado
Marinate for 1 hour in
½ cup lemon juice   **½ teaspoon salt**
Line salad bowl with
Lettuce
When ready to serve, arrange drained cucumbers, peas,
avocado, and decorate with
1 one-lb can sliced pickled beets well drained.

Mandarin Orange Mold

#2   *10 servings*
Drain, reserving juices
2 eleven-oz cans mandarin   **1 thirteen and a half-oz can**
oranges   **crushed pineapple**
Dissolve
3 three-oz packages orange gelatin
in
2 cups boiling water

Add
2 cups fruit juices
Cool and refrigerate until consistency of unbeaten egg
whites. Add

Fruits   1 pint orange sherbet
Mix thoroughly. Place in 12-cup ring mold and jell. Unmold to serve.

Mother's Potato Salad
#2   8 *servings*
Cook in salted water until tender
4 large potatoes
Peel. Slice into a bowl.
Add

1 onion, cut fine   4 strips bacon, fried crisp
5 stalks celery, cut fine   and crumbled
2 hard-cooked eggs, chopped

Mix with following dressing and let stand at least 8 hours:

DRESSING
Combine in order given, stirring after each addition. Boil
until thick. Cool before adding to salad

1 beaten egg   ½ cup vinegar
Scant ½ cup sugar   2 tablespoons butter
1 tablespoon flour   1 teaspoon salt
½ cup water   ¼ teaspoon pepper

Pineapple-Lime Mold
#2   4–6 *servings*
Dissolve
1 three-oz package lime gelatin
in
1 cup hot water
Add

Juice of 1 one-lb four-oz can   Water (if necessary) to
  crushed pineapple   make 1 cup

Combine and add to gelatin

**2 heaping tablespoons sour   Crushed pineapple
cream**

Mix thoroughly. Pour into 1-quart mold. Jell in refrigerator. Unmold.

Salad Colette

#1   *4 servings*

Cook

1 ten-oz package frozen peas

with

1 tablespoon minced dried onion

Drain and chill. Blend

1 teaspoon white horseradish   2 tablespoons sour cream

Add to peas and mix gently. Refrigerate. Serve cold on bed of

Lettuce

Sherry-Cherry Mold

#2   *6 servings*

Drain, reserving syrup

1 one-lb can Bing cherries

Dissolve

1 three-oz package black-cherry gelatin

in

¾ cup hot water

Stir in

½ cup dry sherry   ¾ cup cherry syrup

Chill until consistency of unbeaten egg whites. Add

Cherries   ½ cup sour cream
½ cup blanched almonds

Pour into 1-quart mold. Jell. Unmold.

Spicy Peach-Cranberry Ring

#2   *8 servings*

Especially good and pretty at Thanksgiving.

Drain, reserving syrup

1 one-lb thirteen-oz can cling peach halves

Add enough water to syrup to make 1¾ cups

Add to liquid and simmer uncovered 10 minutes

1 teaspoon whole cloves   ¼ cup vinegar
3-inch stick cinnamon

Add peaches, heat slowly for 5 minutes. Remove peaches. Place in 3-quart ring mold, cut side up. Strain syrup. Measure and add enough hot water to make 1⅔ cups. Add liquid to

2 three-oz packages lemon gelatin

Dissolve and pour over peaches. Refrigerate until almost firm. In the meantime put through food chopper, using medium blade

1 cup fresh or frozen cran-   ½ unpeeled orange
berries

Stir in

⅓ cup sugar

Add

1¾ cups hot water

to

1 three-oz package cherry gelatin

Cool. Add cranberry mixture. Pour over almost jelled peach mixture. Jell. To serve, unmold.

Spinach Salad

#1   *6 servings*

Combine

1 lb spinach leaves, torn in   1 onion, sliced in fine rings
pieces   ¼ lb bleu cheese, crumbled
2 hard-boiled eggs, diced   1 cup mayonnaise
1 red apple, diced, unpeeled   ½ pint sour cream

Serve chilled.

Strawberry-Rhubarb Mold

#2   *6 servings*

Combine

1 one-lb package frozen
   strawberries, defrosted and
   drained

1 one-lb package frozen rhu-
   barb, cooked

1 one-lb four-oz can crushed
   pineapple, drained*

Dissolve

2 three-oz packages strawberry gelatin

in

1 cup boiling water

Combine juices from 3 fruits to make 3 cups liquid, adding water if necessary. Add to gelatin. Chill until slightly
thickened. Add fruits and pour into 2-quart ring mold. Jell.
Unmold to serve.

* Always use canned pineapple—never fresh or frozen—for gelatin
molds or the mold will not jell!

IV: Elegant but Easy
Desserts

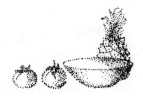

Cakes

Almond Torte

8 *servings*

Beat together until thick

6 egg yolks   1 cup sugar

Add

1 cup grated carrots   ½ lb blanched ground almonds

Fold in

6 stiffly beaten egg whites

Add

1 tablespoon dry sherry

Line bottoms of two 9-inch pans with waxed paper. Pour batter equally into pans. Bake at 350° F for 25 minutes.

Cool. Cake layers may be frozen. Fill layers with
Raspberry jam
Refrigerate. When ready to serve, cover with
½ pint heavy cream, whipped stiff

Applesauce Cake

*#1   *8–10 servings*

Cream

½ cup butter   1 cup sugar

Add and beat to blend

1 egg   **1 teaspoon vanilla**

Then add

1 cup dates, sliced   **¼ teaspoon cloves**
1½ cups applesauce   **2 cups sifted flour**
1 cup walnuts, chopped   **2 teaspoons baking soda**
1 cup raisins   **1 teaspoon salt**
½ teaspoon cinnamon

Bake in bread pan or 10-inch tube pan for 1 hour at
350° F.

Apricot Angel Cake

#1   *8 servings*

Soak overnight
1 eleven-oz package dried apricots
Simmer apricots in soaking water until soft.
Hollow out, leaving 1-inch rim around edge of
1 ten-inch angel food cake (made from packaged mix)
Use these pieces to fill in hole at bottom. Fill center with
½ pint heavy cream, whipped   2 tablespoons sugar
and sweetened with
Dissolve
1 three-oz package orange gelatin
in
1 cup hot water

Add
Drained cooked apricots
Sweeten to taste with sugar. Cool. Pour mixture over whipped cream. Jell.

California Coffee Cake

*#2   *10 servings*

Mix together for filling

½ cup brown sugar, packed	1 tablespoon flour
1 teaspoon cinnamon	½ cup chopped walnuts
1 tablespoon butter, melted	

Cream together

½ cup butter	1 cup sugar

Add

2 egg yolks	2 teaspoons baking powder
1½ cups sifted flour	Grated rind of 1 lemon
1 teaspoon salt	Grated rind of 1 orange

Beat well. Then stir in
½ cup milk
Fold in
2 egg whites stiffly beaten
Pour 4/5 batter into greased 9-inch spring form. Sprinkle on filling mixture. Then spread on rest of batter. Bake at 350° F for 50 minutes. Run knife around edge to remove sides from pan and cool in pan on wire rack.

Cheesecake de Menthe

*#1   *10–12 servings*

CRUST

Combine

1 cup vanilla wafer crumbs	¼ cup brown sugar, firmly packed
	¼ cup melted butter

Press into bottom and sides of 9-inch spring form cake pan. Bake at 350° F for 5 minutes. Chill.

FILLING

Combine in top of double boiler

3 envelopes unflavored gela-   ¾ cup sugar
tin   ¼ teaspoon salt

Stir in

2 egg yolks, slightly beaten   pineapple, add water (if
1 cup juice drained from   necessary) to make 1 cup
1 twenty-oz can crushed

Cook over low heat until slightly thick, about 10 minutes.
Remove from heat and add

2 tablespoons lemon juice

Cool. Stir in

2 cups small curd cottage   ¼ cup crème de menthe
cheese   (green)
                               Pineapple, well drained

Chill. Stir occasionally until mixture is slightly thick.
Beat until stiff

2 egg whites

Fold into gelatin mixture

egg whites   1 cup heavy cream, whipped

Spoon into crumb crust. Chill until firm.

Chocolate Roll

*#1   6–8 servings

Marian's favorite dessert! Her husband's too!

Separate

7 eggs

placing yolks in small mixing bowl and whites in large. Add
to yolks and beat until light, fluffy, and creamy

1 cup sugar

Melt over very low heat

½ lb dark *sweet* chocolate   7 tablespoons coffee

Cool slightly. Meanwhile stiffly beat

Egg whites   Pinch of salt

Combine, by folding, whites, yolks, and chocolate. Oil

10x15-inch jelly-roll pan. Cover with buttered waxed paper. Place mixture in pan and bake at 350° F 15–20 minutes in gas oven, 12 minutes in electric oven. Remove and cool for 5 minutes. Cover with slightly damp cloth and cool completely at room temperature. Place in refrigerator for 1 hour. Remove cloth carefully and sprinkle top generously with
Bitter cocoa

Turn out onto waxed paper. Remove waxed paper from top and spread with mixture of

2 cups heavy cream, whipped   2 tablespoons rum

Roll up very carefully and quickly like jelly roll. This cake will crack as it rolls. It is supposed to resemble the bark of a tree.

Chocolate Syrup Cake

*#2   *8 servings*

Easy enough for a child to make but simply delicious!
Cream together

½ cup butter   1 cup sugar

Add one at a time, beating well after each addition

4 eggs
Add

1 sixteen-oz can chocolate   1 teaspoon vanilla
syrup

Beat. Stir in
1 cup self-rising flour

Bake at 350° F for 45–50 minutes in 9x13 pan well greased and floured. Cool. Sprinkle with
Confectioners' sugar

Coffee-Walnut Roll

*#1   *8 servings*

Preheat oven to 375° F. Butter a 10x15 jelly-roll pan, spread it with buttered waxed paper. Beat until pale

5 egg yolks   ¾ cup sugar

Mix together and stir into yolk mixture

3 tablespoons ground wal-   3 tablespoons instant coffee
nuts   powder

1 tablespoon flour

Whip until stiff

5 egg whites   Pinch of salt

Add gradually, beating until stiff

¼ cup sugar

Fold whites into yolks. Spread in pan and bake 15 minutes. Invert onto cloth sprinkled with

Confectioners' sugar

Peel off paper and roll up cake on its length. Cool, covered with cloth. Combine

2 cups heavy cream,   3 tablespoons sugar
whipped   2 teaspoons vanilla

When cake is cool, unroll it, spread on cream mixture and roll up again. Sprinkle with confectioners' sugar.

Ellen's Cheesecake

*#2   14 servings

Probably everyone else will claim this too after they sample it!

CRUST

Combine

26 graham crackers, rolled   ¾ cup butter
fine, about 1¾ cups   1 tablespoon brown sugar
crumbs

Line bottom of 9-inch spring form with this mixture.

FILLING

Combine and beat at medium speed for 20–25 minutes

24 oz cream cheese   1 cup sugar
4 eggs   1 teaspoon vanilla

Place cheese mixture in spring form. Bake 40 minutes at

325° F. Cool for 35 minutes. While cooling beat together for 10 minutes

1 pint sour cream   ¾ cup sugar

Pour over top of baked cake. Bake at 400° F for 10 minutes—watch carefully. It should brown *very* slightly on top. Refrigerate at least overnight and as Ellen says, "Don't count the calories."

French Orange Cake
*#2   *12–14 servings*
Cream together

1 cup butter   2 cups sugar
Add

½ teaspoon vanilla   2 tablespoons grated orange
                                   rind

Add one at a time, beating well after each addition
5 eggs
Sift together

3 cups cake flour   Pinch salt
1 tablespoon baking powder

Add flour mixture to batter alternately with
¾ cup milk

Spoon into buttered and floured 10-inch tube pan. Bake at 350° F for 1 hour. Cool pan on wire rack for 2 minutes.
Heat in saucepan until sugar is dissolved

¼ cup butter   ⅓ cup orange juice
⅔ cup sugar

Pour evenly over cake in pan while cake is still hot. Allow cake to cool thoroughly in pan before removing.

Fruit Salad Upside-Down Cake
*#2   *8 servings*
In large iron skillet melt
½ cup butter

Spread evenly in pan

1 **cup brown sugar**
Arrange on sugar

1 **one-lb four-oz can "fruits   2 tablespoons pecans
for salad," drained**
Sift together

1 **cup cake flour   ¼ teaspoon salt**
1 **teaspoon baking powder**
Beat until light

3 **egg yolks**
Add gradually

1 **cup granulated sugar**
Add

Syrup from fruit   Sifted flour
Fold in

3 **egg whites, stiffly beaten**
Pour over fruits in pan. Bake at 375° F for 30–35 minutes.
Leave in pan until ready to serve. Before serving warm in
oven for 10 minutes and turn out on cake plate. Serve warm.

Fruit Torte
*#3   *8 servings*

This gets a 10-star rating on our list.
Cream

1 **cup sugar   ½ cup butter**
Add

1 **cup flour, sifted   Salt**
1 **teaspoon baking powder   2 eggs**

Place in 9-inch spring form. Add to top and cover entire
surface with one of the following or a combination of:

1 **pint blueberries   Sliced apples**
24 **halves pitted Italian   Sliced peaches**
plums (skin side up)

(In winter, frozen or canned blueberries or peaches may be substituted. If using canned, drain and wash off syrup well.)

Sprinkle top with

Sugar   Cinnamon (use a heavy
Lemon juice   hand)
Flour (if fruit is very juicy)

Bake at 350° F for one hour. Delicious when served with vanilla ice cream or whipped cream. Best served slightly warm. Refresh in oven, if desired.

Orange-Nut Cake

*#2   *8 servings*
    Cream

½ lb butter   1 cup sugar
    Add
3 egg yolks
    Sift together
2 cups flour, sifted   1 teaspoon baking soda
1 teaspoon baking powder

    Add dry mixture to creamed mixture alternately with
½ pint sour cream
    Stir in
Grated rind of 1 orange   2 tablespoons orange juice
½ cup walnuts, chopped
    Fold in
3 stiffly beaten egg whites

Bake in buttered and lightly floured 10-inch tube pan at 350° F for 1 hour. While cake is still hot and before removing it from pan, spoon over it the following mixture:

½ cup orange juice   1 tablespoon Cointreau
½ cup sugar

    Serve with the following:

ORANGE SAUCE (#2)

Stir over low flame until thick

½ cup orange juice
½ teaspoon grated lemon
   rind
1 teaspoon lemon juice

3 tablespoons sugar
1 beaten egg yolk
1 tablespoon Cointreau

Cool sauce and beat it until foamy. Serve in separate bowl.

Orange Sponge Cake

#2   *8 servings*

Fit for the gods.

Hang upside down until cool

1 sponge cake (You can cheat and buy one but it won't be
as good.) See next recipe.

Beat until stiff

2 egg whites

Add

¼ cup confectioners' sugar   Juice of six oranges
Rind of three oranges, grated

Put ⅓ of this mixture on deep cake plate. Split cake in
half, horizontally. Put cake into cake plate on top of mixture, cut side down. Cover with ⅓ mixture. Top with second
layer of cake. Put last ⅓ of mixture on top of second layer.
Refrigerate overnight. When ready to serve cover with

½ pint heavy cream,   Grated coconut to garnish
   whipped

Sponge Cake with Chocolate Filling

*#1   *8 servings*

Beat

6 egg whites

with

⅛ teaspoon cream of tartar

Gradually add

½ cup sugar

and beat until stiff and glossy.

Beat together

6 egg yolks   ½ cup sugar
Grated rind of ½ lemon   2 tablespoons lemon juice

Fold yolks and whites together. Fold in

1 cup sifted cake flour   1 teaspoon salt
1 teaspoon baking powder,
   sifted

Bake in 10-inch tube pan for 1 hour at 325° F. Freeze or refrigerate. When ready to serve, slice cake in half, horizontally. Fill and top with

CHOCOLATE FILLING

Blend

⅔ cup chocolate syrup   1 beaten egg white
½ pint heavy cream,
   whipped

Strawberry Roll

#2   *8 servings*

Beat until thick and light in color

4 eggs   ¼ teaspoon salt
¾ teaspoon baking powder

Gradually add

¾ cup sugar

Add

1 teaspoon vanilla

Fold in

¾ cup sifted cake flour

Turn into 15½x10½ jelly-roll pan, lined with greased waxed paper. Bake at 400° F for 13 minutes. Turn from pan on a kitchen towel dusted with confectioners' sugar. Remove paper and cut off crisp edges immediately. Roll like jelly roll with towel inside and wrapping around outside. Chill.

FILLING

Cream until fluffy

9 oz cream cheese   3 tablespoons sugar
3 tablespoons Grand
   Marnier

Carefully unroll cake and remove towel. Spread with cheese mixture. Distribute

1 quart strawberries, sliced

over cheese. Reroll. Chill. Serve with

1 sixteen-oz package frozen strawberries, sliced

Vienna Torte

*#1   *8 servings*

Lois' husband's favorite recipe.
Beat together until thick

1 cup sugar	**7 egg yolks**

Beat until stiff

7 egg whites
Mix together

1 tablespoon instant coffee powder	**½ lb grated pecans**

Fold into this mixture whites and yolks, alternately. Bake at 350° F for 20 minutes in two 9-inch pans lined with waxed paper. Freeze if desired. When ready to serve, bring to room temperature, frost top and sides.

FROSTING

Cook together in double boiler

¼ lb marshmallows	**⅔ cup strong coffee**

Refrigerate until cool. Whip

½ pint heavy cream
Fold into marshmallow mixture. Spread between layers and frost top and sides. Refrigerate until ready to serve.

Pies

Pie Crust—To Make (*)

This is the first pie crust we ever tried—it worked—and it has been foolproof ever since.

Sift together

1½ cups sifted enriched   **½ teaspoon salt**
flour

Cut in with pastry blender

½ cup shortening

until pieces are the size of small peas. Sprinkle

4 tablespoons cold water (approximately)

one at a time, over mixture. Mix with fork. Repeat until dough is moistened. It is of good consistency when it does not stick very much to your hands when you begin to form it into a ball. It will handle more easily if chilled for at least ½ hour but can be worked if chilled only 10 minutes.

Form into two balls—one for small top crust and one for larger bottom crust or just one ball for large bottom crust. Flatten ball and roll with floured rolling pin on floured surface to about ¼-inch thickness. If the dough is rolled out on waxed paper it will be even easier to transfer to the pie plate.

Always roll away from the center. If edges split, pinch together.

An empty pie shell should be pricked all over with a fork, covered with buttered waxed paper, then weighted with uncooked beans or rice. Bake at 450° F for 10 minutes, remove waxed paper and weights and bake another 5–10 minutes until lightly brown.

Pie Crust—To Freeze

Pie crust may be frozen unbaked. For a 9-inch pie, roll out dough, trace a circle 11 inches in diameter and cut it out. Place this flat circle of dough on a piece of aluminum foil, backed by cardboard for support. You may stack many of these circles together by placing 2 sheets of aluminum foil between each crust so that they may be removed easily and defrosted individually in less than an hour. They may then be placed in a pie plate and used like any regular crust.

Angel Pie

#2   *8 servings*

MERINGUE SHELL

Beat until stiff

4 egg whites   **1 teaspoon vinegar**
1 teaspoon vanilla

Add slowly

1 cup sugar

Beat until glossy. Bake in greased 10-inch pie plate at 275° F for 1 hour.

FILLING

Cook in top of double boiler until thick

4 egg yolks, beaten   Juice of 2 whole lemons
½ cup sugar

Cool. Fold in

1 cup heavy cream, whipped   2 teaspoons sugar
1 teaspoon vanilla

Place in meringue shell. Refrigerate. When ready to serve, top pie with more whipped cream.

Apricot Pie

#1   *8 servings*

Provide

1 ten-inch baked pie shell

Simmer in saucepan until tender (about 20 minutes)

1 eleven-oz box dried apri- Juice of one orange
cots   1 stick cinnamon
Juice of one lemon

Meanwhile dissolve

1 envelope gelatin

in

1¾ cups cold water

Heat just to boiling point. Remove cinnamon; purée apricots in blender. Stir in gelatin. Chill until just beginning to set, then beat until frothy. Combine and fold in

2 egg whites, beaten stiff   2 tablespoons sugar

Fold in

½ cup heavy cream, whipped

Pour into pie shell. Chill. Serve topped with

Whipped Cream

Banana Gem Pie

#2   *6–8 servings*

Provide

1 nine-inch baked pie shell

Prepare according to package directions
1 four ¾-oz package raspberry Danish dessert
but using 1½ cups water. Stir in
½ cup red port wine
Cool, stirring occasionally, until lukewarm. Blend

8 oz cream cheese	**⅛ teaspoon nutmeg**
1 tablespoon milk	**⅛ teaspoon vanilla**
¼ cup sugar	**Dash salt**

With teaspoon spread cheese mixture over bottom and
up sides of pie shell. Slice into gelatin mixture
3 medium bananas
Spoon into shell. Refrigerate. Before serving, top with

1 cup heavy cream, whipped   Toasted coconut for garnish

Black Bottom Pie

#2   *6 servings*
Provide
1 eight-inch baked pie shell or graham-cracker crust
Into
¼ cup cold water
Sprinkle
2 teaspoons gelatin
Make custard by cooking and stirring until it coats a spoon

3 egg yolks, beaten	**½ cup sugar**
1 cup milk	**¼ teaspoon salt**

Stir in gelatin. Meanwhile beat until stiff
3 egg whites
Divide custard mixture in half. To one half add

1½ squares unsweetened	**½ teaspoon vanilla**
chocolate, melted	**Half of egg white mixture**

To other half add

3 tablespoons rum   Remainder of egg whites

Cool, and as mixture begins to thicken pour chocolate part
into pie shell.

Cover with rum-flavored custard. Top with layer of
½ pint heavy cream, whipped
Sprinkle with
Unsweetened chocolate shavings

Cherry Chiffon Pie

#2   *10 servings*
Lovely in the summer and really a mile high!

CRUST

Roll into fine crumbs
20 graham crackers or 1⅓ cups crumbs
Add

¼ cup melted butter   ¼ cup sugar
Press into bottom and sides of 10-inch pie plate, reserving
¼ cup crumbs. Bake 8 minutes at 375° F. Cool.

FILLING

Drain juice from
1 one-lb can sour pitted red cherries
Add to juice enough
Water
to make 1 cup. Bring juice to boil. Pour hot juice over
1 three-oz package cherry-flavored gelatin
Stir until dissolved. Add
1 tablespoon lemon juice
Chill until consistency of unbeaten egg whites.
Fluff
6 oz cream cheese
with

**¼ cup medium or heavy   2 tablespoons sugar
cream**
Beat chilled gelatin until frothy. Whip
1¾ cups medium or heavy cream
Fold cream and cherries into gelatin mixture along with
½ teaspoon almond extract
Place ⅓ cherry mixture in shell. Spoon on half of cheese

mixture. Top with half of remaining cherry filling. Spoon on rest of cheese and top with rest of filling. Sprinkle on remaining crumbs. Chill.

Connecticut Pie

#2   *6 servings*

LEMON-CRUMB CRUST

Combine

1¼ cups vanilla wafer crumbs

1½ teaspoons lemon rind, grated

1 tablespoon sugar

¼ cup melted butter or margarine

Press into bottom and sides of 9-inch pie plate.

FILLING

Mix together

1 one-lb fourteen-oz can fruit cocktail, drained

1 pint sour cream

Place mixture in pie shell. Bake at 350° F for 20 minutes. Chill. When ready to serve, top with

Whipped cream   Sprinkle of nutmeg

Double Chocolate Pie

#2   *8 servings*

Mix together

1¼ cups chocolate wafer crumbs

¼ cup sugar

⅓ cup melted butter

Press into bottom and sides of 10-inch pie plate. Bake at 400° F for 5 minutes. Chill.

FILLING

Melt in top of double boiler

1 six-oz package chocolate bits

Remove from heat. Beat in

1 egg

2 egg yolks

1½ teaspoons dark rum

Fold in

2 egg whites, stiffly beaten   1 cup whipped cream

Fill pie shell. Refrigerate. When ready to serve, top with

Whipped cream   ½ square bitter chocolate,
                                               shaved

Down South Pecan Pie

*#1   8 servings

Cream

½ cup butter   ½ cup sugar

Add

¾ cup light corn syrup   1 teaspoon vanilla
2 tablespoons honey   ½ teaspoon salt
3 eggs, slightly beaten   ½ cup pecans

Pour into

Unbaked 9-inch pie shell

Cover with

½ cup pecans

Bake at 350° F for 55 minutes. To serve, top with

½ pint heavy cream, whipped

Grasshopper Pie

#2   Two 11-inch pies—18 servings

Contrary to what Michael Burros thinks, there are NO
grasshoppers in this pie!

Mix together in top of double boiler

3 envelopes gelatin   ⅜ teaspoon salt
¾ cup sugar

Stir in

1½ cups cold water

Blend in, one at a time

9 egg yolks

Place over boiling water, stir until mixture thickens slightly (4–5 minutes). Remove from heat and add

¾ cup green crème de menthe

¾ cup white crème de cacao

Chill until consistency of unbeaten egg whites.
Beat until stiff

9 egg whites

Gradually add

¾ cup sugar

and beat until stiff and glossy.
Fold in gelatin mixture and

2 cups heavy cream, whipped

Green food coloring (to make a very light shade of green)

Turn into

Chocolate crumb shells (double the recipe under Double Chocolate Pie, p. 164)

Chill until firm. If desired, garnish with

Additional whipped cream   Chopped pistachio nuts
Chocolate crumbs

Halloween Surprise Pie

#1   10 *servings*

Good all year long.

CRUST (*)

Cut or rub

½ cup shortening

into

1½ cups sifted *enriched self-rising* flour

until crumbly. Sprinkle with

4 tablespoons cold water

Mix lightly until dough sticks together. If it is too sticky add a bit of flour. Refrigerate for 20 minutes or more to facilitate handling. Turn out on lightly floured board and roll to about ⅛ inch thick. Fit into 11-inch pie plate and flute edge. Prick all over bottom and sides. Fit a piece of buttered waxed paper into pie shell and weight down with beans or rice to prevent bottom from puffing up. Bake at 450° F for 12 minutes. Remove waxed paper and weights. Bake about 5 minutes more until lightly browned. Cool. Freeze if desired. For serving fill with following.

FILLING

Soften

2 envelopes gelatin

in

½ cup cold water

Scald in top of double boiler

1½ cups milk

Mix together

6 egg yolks   ½ cup sugar

Blend a small amount of scalded milk into yolks and return all to milk in double boiler, stirring. Cook over hot, but not boiling, water about 15 minutes, until thickened. Remove and stir in gelatin. Blend in

1 twelve-oz can defrosted orange juice concentrate (undiluted)

Chill until partially set. Beat until frothy

6 egg whites

Gradually beat in

½ cup sugar

until peaks form. Fold into gelatin mixture. Whip

1 cup heavy cream

Fold into gelatin. Spread ⅓ of mixture in cooled pie shell. Sprinkle with

½ of eight-oz sweet chocolate, shaved

Add half of remaining filling. Top with most of remaining chocolate saving enough to decorate top. Top with remaining filling. Decorate with chocolate and refrigerate until serving.

Key Lime Pie

#1   *6 servings*

As cool as an ocean breeze.

LEMON-CRUMB CRUST (See recipe, p. 164)

FILLING

Thoroughly mix in saucepan

1 envelope gelatin	**¼ teaspoon salt**
½ cup sugar	

Beat together

4 egg yolks	**¼ cup water**
½ cup lime juice	

Stir into gelatin mixture. Cook over medium heat, stirring, just until mixture comes to boil. Remove from heat. Stir in

1 teaspoon grated lime peel   **Green food coloring—only enough to give *pale* green color**

Chill stirring occasionally until mixture mounds slightly when dropped from spoon. Beat until soft peaks form

4 egg whites

Gradually add

½ cup sugar

beating until stiff. Fold in gelatin mixture. Fold in

1 cup heavy cream, whipped

Pile into shell. Chill until firm. Before serving top with

Additional whipped cream

Trim with

Lime peel, grated

Macaroon Pie

*#1   *8 servings*

A *startling but effective combination.*

Mix

16 single square saltine crackers, rolled fine	**16 dates, cut up fine**
	½ cup pecans, chopped
	1 cup sugar

Beat together until stiff, but not dry

¼ teaspoon baking powder	**3 egg whites**

Fold egg-white mixture into dry mixture, then pour into

well-buttered 9-inch pie plate. Bake at 350° F for 30 minutes. Freeze or refrigerate. When ready to serve, top with whipped cream.

Mocha Chiffon Pie

*#2   *8 servings*

In a 9-inch pie plate, combine and press to sides and bottom

| 1⅓ cups graham cracker | ¼ cup brown sugar |
| crumbs | ⅓ cup melted butter |

Refrigerate. Meanwhile in top of double boiler pour

¾ cup water
Add
1 envelope unflavored gelatin
Add

| 1 square unsweetened choco- | 2 tablespoons instant coffee |
| late | powder |

Heat until chocolate melts. Beat together

| 3 egg yolks | ½ cup sugar |

Pour mocha mixture over yolks. Beat thoroughly. Refrigerate until it begins to set (about 20 minutes). Now whip until stiff

½ cup heavy cream
Fold into mocha. Whip until they stand in peaks
3 egg whites
Fold into mixture. Pour into crust. Refrigerate until set. Freeze if desired. Thaw in refrigerator for 24 hours. When ready to serve, top with whipped cream.

Pineapple Bavarian Pie

#1   *8 servings*

COCONUT CRUST

Combine in 9-inch pie plate

| ¼ cup butter | 2 cups grated coconut |

Bake at 300° F for 25 minutes. Cool.

FILLING

Drain but save syrup from

1 one-lb four and a half-oz can crushed pineapple

Add to syrup

Water (if necessary) to measure 1½ cups

Sprinkle 1 cup liquid and let stand 5 minutes on

2 envelopes gelatin

In small saucepan combine

½ cup liquid	**1 tablespoon lemon juice**
½ cup sugar	**½ teaspoon salt**

Heat until sugar is dissolved. Pour into gelatin. Stir until it dissolves. Beat well

3 egg yolks

Stir into hot mixture. Refrigerate 30–40 minutes until it thickens to consistency of unbeaten egg whites. Beat until stiff and fold in

3 egg whites

Whip and fold in

¾ cup heavy cream

Pour into crust. Refrigerate at least one hour before serving.

Pumpkin Chiffon Pie

*#2   *8 servings*

Out of this world—you'd never know it's pumpkin.

GINGERSNAP CRUST

Combine

1⅔ cups gingersnap crumbs	**¼ cup melted butter**
(about 22 gingersnaps)	**¼ cup sugar**

Press into bottom and sides of 9-inch pie plate.

FILLING

Cook in top of double boiler for 10 minutes

1 cup canned or cooked pumpkin

Add

4 egg yolks   ½ teaspoon ginger
½ cup sugar   ¼ teaspoon nutmeg
1 cup milk   1 teaspoon cinnamon
½ teaspoon salt   2 tablespoons butter

Stir and cook until of custard consistency. Remove from heat. Add
1 envelope unflavored gelatin
which has been softened in
¼ cup cold water

Chill. When mixture begins to thicken, fold in
4 egg whites, stiffly beaten with ½ cup sugar

Pour into crust. Chill or freeze. Serve topped with
Whipped cream

Strawberry-Cheese Pie

#2   10–14 *servings*

No calorie watchers here, please. A little goes a long way!
Provide
1 eleven-inch graham-cracker crust baked 10 minutes. See recipe, p. 163
Beat in mixer
2 eggs
Add and blend well

16 oz cream cheese   Dash salt
3 heaping tablespoons sour   ¾ cup sugar
   cream   1 teaspoon vanilla

Place in pie shell and bake at 375° F for 20 minutes. Remove from oven and pour over it
½ pint sour cream
which has been mixed with

2 tablespoons sugar   Sprinkle of lemon juice
1 teaspoon vanilla

Bake at 425° F for 5 minutes. Cool. Refrigerate overnight. Bring to boil
1 sixteen-oz package frozen strawberries

in
¼ cup water
that has been thickened with
½ tablespoon cornstarch
   Cool. Save some of mixture for glazing strawberries. Pour remaining mixture over pie. Place
Whole strawberries
on pie and pour on glaze.

Cookies and Small Cakes

Apricot Sticks

*#3   4 *dozen*

Cream together

½ cup butter   1 teaspoon lemon rind,
½ cup sugar   grated

Add one at a time beating after each addition

2 egg yolks

Add

1 cup flour sifted   ¼ teaspoon baking soda
½ teaspoon salt

Spread the dough in a greased 9x13 pan. Cover with
1½ cups thick apricot jam

Beat until stiff

2 egg whites

Gradually add

Fold in

¼ cup sugar

½ cup chopped nuts

Spread meringue over jam. Bake at 350° F for 45 minutes. Cool. Cut into strips. Sprinkle with
Confectioners' sugar

Barbara's Brownies

*#2   12 *large or 16 small ones*

Melt together in double boiler

½ lb butter

4 squares unsweetened chocolate

Cream

2 cups sugar

4 eggs

Combine butter and chocolate with eggs and sugar. Add

2 teaspoons vanilla

1 cup chopped nuts

1 cup flour

Bake at 350° F for 30–40 minutes in 9x13 pan. Should be quite wet after baking for really moist brownies. Use half recipe for 8-inch square pan.

Bonbons

*#3   50 *pieces*

Put through food chopper twice

1 lb pitted dates

½ lb walnut meats

Shape into 50 small balls. Beat stiff

3 egg whites

Gradually add

¾ cup sugar

1 teaspoon vanilla

With teaspoon, roll date balls in meringue. Put on buttered cookie sheets. Bake at 250° F for 30 minutes. Store in airtight container or freeze, if desired.

Chocolate-Coconut Macaroons

*#2   3 *dozen*

Beat until stiff

3 egg whites

Fold into whites

1 six-oz package chocolate   1 teaspoon vanilla
  bits (melted over double   1 three and a half-oz package
  boiler)   shredded coconut

½ cup sugar

Drop onto cookie sheet covered with ungreased brown paper and bake at 375° F for 15–20 minutes.

Icebox Ginger Cookies

*#3   6 *dozen*

Melt

1 cup butter

Pour it over

1 cup sugar

Mix. Heat and add

½ cup molasses

Add

1 teaspoon baking soda   1 teaspoon salt
2 teaspoons ginger   2½ cups sifted flour
1 teaspoon vanilla

Mix all ingredients well. Form into two rolls. Wrap in waxed paper. Chill well in refrigerator. Slice thin and bake at 400° F for 8–9 minutes, on well-greased cookie sheet.

Marble Squares

*#3   2 *dozen squares*

Sift together

1 cup plus 2 tablespoons   ½ teaspoon baking soda
  flour, sifted   ½ teaspoon salt

Blend

½ cup butter
6 tablespoons granulated
sugar

6 tablespoons brown sugar
½ teaspoon vanilla
¼ teaspoon water

Beat in

1 egg

Mix in flour mixture. Stir in

½ cup walnuts, chopped

Spread in greased 9x13 pan. Sprinkle over batter

1 cup chocolate bits

Place in 375° F oven 1 minute. Swirl knife through batter
to marbelize. Bake at 375° F for 12–14 minutes.

Mexican Wedding Cakes

*#3   2 dozen

Cream

3 tablespoons confection-
ers' sugar

½ cup butter

Add

1 cup sliced blanched
almonds

1 teaspoon almond extract

Add and mix in a little at a time

1 cup cake flour

Form into balls. Bake at 325° F for 10–12 minutes.
While warm, roll in

Confectioners' sugar

Mock Strudel

*#3   40 pieces

Mix together

½ lb melted butter
1 tablespoon sugar
¾ teaspoon salt

1 cup sour cream
2¼ cups flour, sifted

Stir mixture until it forms a ball. Roll in waxed paper and
refrigerate for an hour. Cut into four equal parts. Roll out
each on floured waxed paper to form a rectangle.

Combine

Six-oz orange marmalade   **Six-oz apricot preserves**

Spread equally on four rectangles. Combine

½ cup brown sugar   **1 cup chopped walnuts**
1 tablespoon cinnamon   **½ cup white raisins**

Divide mixture into four equal parts.

Sprinkle mixture over four rectangles. Then roll up each as for jelly roll and place on greased, floured cookie sheet. Bake at 325° F for one hour. Sprinkle with

Confectioners' sugar

When cool, cut each roll into 10 pieces.

Orange Tea Cookies

*#3   *4–5 dozen*

Cream together

¼ lb butter   **⅓ cup sugar**
1 egg yolk

Blend in

1 cup sifted flour   **Pinch salt**
½ teaspoon vanilla

Add

**1 tablespoon orange rind,   1 tablespoon lemon rind,
grated   grated**

Mix. Using ½ teaspoon of mixture, shape into balls. Roll in

1 unbeaten egg white

Then roll in

2 cups walnuts, chopped

Place on well greased cookie sheet. Pat down to thin cookie. Bake at 350° F for 12 minutes.

Pecan Drops

*#3   *4–5 dozen*

Mix

½ cup butter   **½ cup plus 2 tablespoons
                                    shortening**

Beat in

1 cup chopped pecans   2½ cups sifted cake flour
1 cup confectioners' sugar   2 teaspoons vanilla

Mix well and drop by teaspoonfuls onto greased cookie sheets. Bake at 325° F for 15–20 minutes.

Raspberry (or Apricot) Dreams

*#3   5 dozen

Sift together

1 cup flour, sifted   Pinch salt
1 teaspoon baking powder

Add

½ cup butter   1 tablespoon milk
1 egg, beaten

Beat until smooth. Roll or pat out in 10x15 pan. Spread thinly with

12 oz raspberry jam or 12 oz apricot jam

Then spread following mixture over jam:

⅛ lb butter, melted   1½ cups coconut
1 cup sugar   1 egg, beaten

Bake at 325° F for 25 minutes. Cut into squares or diamonds.

Russian Tea Cookies

*#3   4 dozen

Mix

1 cup soft butter   1 teaspoon vanilla
½ cup confectioners' sugar

Sift together and add to above

2¼ cups flour, sifted   ¼ teaspoon salt

Add

¾ cup finely chopped walnuts

Chill in freezer for ½ hour until dough is easily handled. Roll into 1-inch balls. Place 2 inches apart on ungreased

baking sheet. Bake at 400° F only until set—do not brown—
8–10 minutes in electric oven, 10–12 minutes in gas oven.
While warm, roll in
Confectioners' sugar
Cool. Roll in sugar again.

Toffee Squares with Chocolate Topping
*#2   *40 squares*
Cream until fluffy

1 cup butter   **1 cup light brown sugar**
Beat in

1 egg yolk   **1 teaspoon vanilla**
Stir in

2 cups sifted flour
Spread thinly in 9x13 pan. Bake at 350° F for 15–20
minutes.
Melt in top of double boiler

6 oz semisweet chocolate
Spread on cookie surface while warm. Sprinkle with

1 cup walnuts, chopped
Cut into squares when cool.

Just for fun make Fruit Torte (p. 154) or Macaroon
Pie (p. 168) in smallest muffin tins and bake about 25–30
minutes at temperatures given in recipes. These finger-sized
desserts are excellent for buffet service and are especially
attractive if tins are lined with the miniature muffin papers.
Put a dab of whipped cream on each macaroon miniature.

Fruit Desserts

Baked Fruit Compote

#1   *12 servings*

Excellent served hot with poultry too.
Drain thoroughly retaining syrups

1 one-lb thirteen-oz can peach halves

1 one-lb fourteen-oz can pitted apricots

1 one-lb fourteen-oz can pineapple chunks

1 one-lb thirteen-oz can pear halves

2 one-lb cans pitted Bing cherries

1 cup frozen raspberries or strawberries, defrosted

In large casserole place each fruit in layers, sprinkling each layer with

Brown sugar   **Lemon**
Cinnamon
Dot with
Butter
Sprinkle with
Cointreau

Bake 45 minutes at 350° F. Mix together

¾ cup fruit syrups   **⅓ cup cornstarch**

Add to baked fruit and return to oven for 15 minutes more. Serve hot. If prepared in advance, refrigerate until ready to serve, then reheat at 350° F for 10–15 minutes.

Banane Flambé

Make at the table. A quickie.
For each serving, heat

1½ oz crème de cacao   **1½ oz white rum**
In chafing dish melt

1 pat butter   **1 tablespoon honey**
Add
½ banana

Spoon sauce over banana and warm. Add liqueurs and flame.

Cherries Jubilee

8 servings

It is effective to make the entire dessert at the table.
In chafing dish over direct heat melt—stirring gently
¾ cup currant jelly
Add
2 one-lb cans pitted Bing cherries, drained

Heat slowly until simmering. Pour into center of fruit, but do not stir
½ cup brandy

Let it heat, then light carefully with match. Immediately spoon over individual portions of previously balled
1½ quarts vanilla ice cream

Fruit Fiesta

#2   *8–10 servings*

In baking dish arrange in alternate layers

1 one-lb can grapefruit sections

1 one-lb can pears

1 one-lb four-oz can pineapple chunks

10 maraschino cherries

½ cup dark brown sugar

1 tablespoon (or more) curry powder

Pour over this

¼ lb melted butter

Bake at 300° F for one hour. Let stand at least 6 hours. After this it should be refrigerated. To serve, reheat at 300° F for about 45 minutes.

Macédoine of Fruit

#2   *6 servings*

Combine and let stand in refrigerator for one hour

½ cup dry vermouth

¼ cup sugar

¼ teaspoon cinnamon

Strain liquid and discard sugar residue. Pour liquid over following prepared fresh fruit

1 medium pineapple, cut in wedges

3 navel oranges, peeled and sectioned

18 large grapes, halved and seeded

Marinate at least one hour in refrigerator before serving.

Melon-Mint Cups

#1   *6 servings*

Boil for 5 minutes

½ cup water

½ cup sugar

Pour syrup over

3 tablespoons mint leaves, well-chopped

or

2 teaspoons mint extract

Cool. Strain. Add

Juice of 1 lemon   Juice of 1 orange

Chill. Just before serving, pour over melon balls cut from

2 cantaloupes   1 honeydew

Pineapple Surprise

½ pineapple per person

Oh's and ah's are worth the little bit of last minute work.

Halve lengthwise

Small pineapples

Scoop out shells, cutting meat into small pieces. Sugar inside of shells, if desired. Cover leaves with aluminum foil. Replace most of pineapple in shells. When ready to serve, place in each half

Large scoop vanilla ice cream

Prepare meringue by beating until stiff

1 egg white for each serving   1 tablespoon sugar for each serving

Cover surfaces of ice cream and pineapple completely with

Meringue

Bake at 400° F for 6 minutes or until meringue is browned. Serve immediately.

Purple-Plum Crunch

#2   *6 servings*

In bottom of shallow 2-quart ungreased baking dish place

24 Italian plums, pitted and quartered

Sprinkle with mixture of

¼ cup brown sugar   ½ teaspoon cinnamon

3 tablespoons flour

Mix thoroughly, using fork. Prepare topping by mixing

1 cup granulated sugar ¼ teaspoon salt
1 teaspoon baking powder 1 egg, well beaten
1 cup flour, sifted

Sprinkle evenly over plums. Over this pour

½ cup butter, melted

When ready to serve, bake at 375° F for 45 minutes.

Raspberry-Filled Melon

#2   *4 servings*

Stir

1 tablespoon cornstarch

into

1 tablespoon water

Add

1 sixteen-oz package frozen   1 small sprig fresh mint
   raspberries or strawberries   Few grains of salt
½ cup red currant jelly

Bring to a boil. Lower heat and simmer 5 minutes. Remove mint, press berries through sieve and discard seeds. Chill.

Cut in half and remove seeds from

2 small cantaloupes

Cut thin slice from bottom so melon will sit flat. Using melon ball cutter, scoop balls from rim of melon, pile in center of melon half. Fill holes and center with sauce.

Strawberry-Raspberry Supreme

#1   *4–6 servings*

Wash, hull, and lightly sugar

1 pint strawberries

Partially thaw

1 sixteen-oz package frozen raspberries

When berries are still slightly crystallized, work through sieve, or, easier still, blend in blender. Spoon strawberries into serving dish, pour raspberry purée over top and chill. Serve with whipped cream.

Tropical Salad

#2   *10 servings*

Mix together

1 four-oz can coconut

2 ten-oz cans mandarin oranges, well drained

1 fourteen-oz can crushed pineapple, drained

1 pint sour cream

16 marshmallows cut in quarters or 64 miniatures

Place in 2-quart mold and refrigerate at least 24 hours before serving. Unmold and serve.

Refrigerator and Freezer Desserts

Apricot Layer Loaf

6–8 servings

Surprise inside!

Start with very hard frozen

2 packages brick (1 quart) vanilla ice cream

Split each brick in half, making 4 layers. Between layers and over entire loaf spread

1 recipe apricot sauce (see below)

Return to freezer until sauce is firm. Then frost loaf with

1 cup whipped cream

Garnish with

¼ cup walnuts, chopped

Place in freezer for at least 1 hour.

APRICOT SAUCE

Purée—use blender for ease

1 cup stewed apricots (follow package directions for cooking)

Add

¼ teaspoon salt   1 tablespoon lemon juice

2 tablespoons sugar   2 teaspoons brandy

After combining all ingredients, chill before spreading on loaf.

Bavarian Cream with Liqueur

#1   6 *servings*

In

2 tablespoons cold water

Soften

1 envelope gelatin

Combine until smooth and creamy

4 egg yolks   ½ cup sugar

Scald

1 cup milk

Pour milk gradually over yolk mixture, stirring. Cook over boiling water, stirring until smooth and thick. Add gelatin, and stir until dissolved. Cool. Stir often to prevent crust from forming. Add

3 tablespoons any liqueur such as Cointreau or crème de cacao

Fold in

1 cup heavy cream, whipped

Pour into individual dishes or one large one. Refrigerate till firm.

Carrot Soufflé

#2   *8 servings*

Mix together

1 cup sugar

6 egg yolks

1 cup cooked carrots, mashed (almost 1 lb) or use strained baby food carrots

2 tablespoons orange juice

1 tablespoon lemon juice

1 cup blanched almonds, grated (measure after grating)

Fold in

6 egg whites, stiffly beaten

Pour into 2½-quart soufflé dish. Bake at 350° F for 45 minutes. Allow to cool. Then spread on a layer of

raspberry jam or preserves

Cover with

1 cup heavy cream, whipped

Chocolate-Coconut Mousse

#2   *6 servings*

Soften

1 envelope gelatin

in

1½ cups cold milk

Add

⅓ cup sugar

¼ teaspoon salt

2 squares unsweetened chocolate

Cook in top of double boiler until chocolate melts and gelatin dissolves. Pour over

3 egg yolks, beaten

Cook and stir 3 minutes longer. Cool 10 minutes. Beat until stiff

3 egg whites

Add

⅓ cup sugar

Fold into chocolate mixture. Add

1 teaspoon vanilla   ½ cup coconut (reserve remainder of 3½-oz box)

Turn into 1-quart mold. Chill overnight. Unmold and cover with mixture of

½ cup heavy cream,   3 tablespoons cocoa
whipped stiff

Top with
Remainder of box of coconut

Coffee Mallow

#2   *6 servings*

Layers range from coffee color to almost white.
Cut into quarters, using scissors
32 marshmallows (do not use miniatures)
Prepare and bring to a boil
1 cup strong coffee
Pour boiling coffee over marshmallows. Fold in
1 cup heavy cream, whipped stiff
Pour into parfait glasses. Let cool at room temperature for 30 minutes, then refrigerate at least 4 hours before serving.

Cold Lemon Soufflé

#1   *8–10 servings*

Pour
2 cups boiling water
over
1 six-oz package lemon gelatin
Stir until dissolved. Add

2 seven-oz bottles lemon-   **Rind of one lemon, grated**
lime carbonated drink   **Juice of one lemon**

Chill until slightly thick then beat until foamy. Fold in
2 cups heavy cream, whipped
Turn into 2-quart soufflé dish. Chill until firm. Serve with
Fresh strawberries or raspberries

Colettes

*   12 *servings*

Melt in top of double boiler

| 12 squares semisweet | ¼ cup butter |
| chocolate | |

Remove from heat and add

½ teaspoon vanilla

Let thicken slightly. Coat inside of 2 thicknesses of fluted paper cups with chocolate about ⅛-inch thick or less, using a spoon or your finger. Place in muffin tins. Chill in freezer a few minutes and remove to fill in any thin places or holes. Freeze firm. Carefully remove paper from chocolate cases and fill with

| Liqueur-flavored whipped | Vanilla mousse (see below) |
| cream or | |

Freeze firm. To serve, defrost about 15 minutes.

VANILLA MOUSSE

Whip

2 cups heavy cream

Add

4 tablespoons confectioners'	1 teaspoon vanilla extract or
sugar	One-inch scraped vanilla
	bean

Spoon into chocolate cases and freeze firm.

Crème Brûlée

#1   4 *servings*

An easy French custard with unusual flavor.

Stir constantly, bring to boiling point and boil exactly 1 minute

1 pint heavy cream

Remove from heat. In a slow steady stream pour it into

4 well-beaten egg yolks

beating constantly. Return to heat. Cook over low heat, stirring, until nearly boiling. Pour into greased baking dish.

Chill well. Cover top with
⅓-inch layer of brown sugar
Place dish in pan of ice cubes and place it under a broiler
6 to 8 inches from heat (keeping oven door open) to form
a crust and carmelize sugar. Watch it very carefully because
it can burn very quickly. Chill again and serve cold.

Crème Renversée au Caramel
#1   *8 servings*
Considered the "crème de la crème" of custards.
Cook over medium heat, stirring until carmelized
1 cup sugar
Add and stir until smooth
½ cup water
Pour mixture, which should be like corn syrup, into 1-quart
ring mold. Rotate to coat bottom and lower sides. Let it set.
Beat together, until blended but not foamy

4 whole eggs	**⅓ cup sugar**
4 egg yolks	**⅛ teaspoon salt**
Scald	

1 cup heavy cream	**1-inch scraped vanilla bean**
2½ cups milk	

Add to egg mixture. You may strain the mixture. Then
pour, a little at a time into prepared ring mold. Set mold in
pan of boiling water and bake at 325° F for 45 minutes.
Remove and set mold in cold water to cool quickly. Chill.
When ready to serve, unmold by running knife around inner
and outer rims of mold. Invert on serving plate. Shake gently
and lift off mold. Fill center with
Whipped cream

Do-It-Yourself Sundaes
Place bowl of ice cream balls on table with dishes of
**Nuts, coconut, whipped cream, cherries and one or more of
the following sauces**

HOT CHERRY SAUCE

#3   *8 servings*

Drain, reserving syrup

1 one-lb can pitted Bing   1 one-lb can light sweet
cherries   cherries

Combine

Syrups   2 tablespoons orange rind,
1 cup sugar   grated
                                  3 tablespoons cornstarch

Bring to a boil, stirring; cook until thick. Stir in cherries.
Reheat to serve.

HOT FUDGE SAUCE

#3   *8 servings*

Mix together

1½ cups sugar   1 cup cocoa
Dash salt

Add

1 cup hot water
Bring to a boil and stir for 3 minutes. Add

2 teaspoons vanilla
Refrigerate. Reheat to serve.

PEAR AND ORANGE SAUCE

#3   *8 servings*

Pare, halve, and core

4 pears
Combine and bring to a boil

½ cup sugar   ¼ cup water
¼ cup orange juice

Add pears and simmer about 20 minutes. Remove fruit.
Add

1 tablespoon orange rind, grated
Simmer 3–5 minutes. Return fruit to sauce. Chill.

CRÈME DE MENTHE

Don't overlook the obvious. Crème de menthe makes a

delicious topping for lemon sherbet. This is particularly good after a heavy meal.

Eleanor's Blueberry Mousse

#1   *8 servings*

Drain, reserving syrup
2 fifteen-oz cans wild blueberries
Put syrup in top of double boiler with
¼ cup quick-cooking tapioca   Juice of 3 lemons

Stir until blended. Cover and cook over medium heat. Stir occasionally until tapioca swells and mixture is smooth and thick. Remove to mixing bowl. Cool. Add drained berries carefully. Soak for 5 minutes
2 tablespoons gelatin
in
½ cup water

Set cup of gelatin in small pan of hot water over low heat until gelatin dissolves. Add to blueberry mixture and stir. Whip stiff and fold into blueberry mixture
½ cup heavy cream
Beat stiff and fold into mixture
4 egg whites

Pour into cold, rinsed ring mold. Refrigerate. Anytime within 5 hours of serving, unmold. Drain
1 fifteen-oz can wild blueberries
Beat till stiff
1½ cups heavy cream
Sweeten with
½ cup confectioners' sugar
Flavor with
1 tablespoon vanilla

Decorate mold with whipped cream and drained blueberries.

Frozen Lemon Pie

*   *8–10 servings*

WAFER CRUST

Combine

1¼ cups vanilla wafer   ¼ cup melted butter
crumbs

Press on bottom and sides of 10-inch pie plate.

FILLING

In top of double boiler combine

3 egg yolks   ¼ cup lemon juice
1 scant cup sugar   Grated rind of 1 lemon

Cook until thick. Cool. Fold in

3 egg whites, beaten stiff   1 cup heavy cream, whipped

Pour filling into crumb crust. Freeze until firm. Remove
from freezer. Let stand in refrigerator for 20 minutes before
serving.

Grand Marnier Soufflé Froid

#2   *10–12 servings*

In saucepan stir smooth

½ cup sugar   2 tablespoons lemon juice
1 cup water   1 envelope plus 2 teaspoons
½ cup Grand Marnier   gelatin
liqueur   7 egg yolks

Cook over low heat, stirring until mixture coats the spoon.
Transfer to large bowl and refrigerate until the consistency
of unbeaten egg whites. Make a collar to fit around a 2-quart
soufflé dish: fold a 30-inch length of waxed paper in half
lengthwise and butter one side of strip. Wrap, buttered side
in, around soufflé dish so that collar stands 3 inches above
rim.

Dribble

2–3 tablespoons Grand Marnier

over

1 two-and-three-fourths-oz package lady fingers

Line sides of soufflé dish with the lady fingers.
Into cooled gelatin mixture fold

¾ cup slivered blanched almonds
Whip

2 cups heavy cream
Beat until soft peaks form

7 egg whites   **¼ teaspoon salt**
While beating stiff, gradually add

¼ cup sugar
Fold both whites and cream into gelatin mixture and turn into soufflé dish. Refrigerate. To serve sprinkle on top of soufflé.

¼ cup slivered almonds

Ice-Cream Bonbons

*   *6–8 servings*
Form into balls with melon ball cutter

1 quart vanilla ice cream
Roll balls in

1 seven and a half-oz can salted peanuts, chopped very fine
Freeze until firm. Quickly dip balls into following sauce. Refreeze for at least one hour.

CHOCOLATE SAUCE (*#3)
Melt in top of double boiler

6 squares unsweetened   **⅔ cup water**
  chocolate
Add

1⅓ cups sugar
Boil gently over direct heat for 4 minutes, stirring constantly.
Remove from heat and stir in

¼ cup butter
Keep warm over hot water while dipping, reheating if necessary. This sauce is an excellent topping for other desserts, either hot or cold.

Ice-Cream Surprise

*   *8–10 servings*

Mix together

1 gallon softened vanilla ice
cream
1 six-oz can frozen lemonade
concentrate, defrosted

1 twelve-oz jar apricot
preserves

Freeze.

Lemon-Angel Trifle

#2   *8 servings*

Break into walnut-sized pieces
1 ten-inch angel food cake (made from packaged mix)
Sprinkle
1 envelope gelatin
on
½ cup cold water
Cook over hot water, stirring until thick

¾ cup lemon juice
¾ cup sugar
6 egg yolks

2 tablespoons lemon rind,
grated

Stir in gelatin mixture. Set aside to cool. Beat until foamy
6 egg whites
Add gradually
¾ cup sugar
beating until stiff. Fold in cooled mixture and cake pieces.
Place in 9-inch spring form. Refrigerate overnight. When
ready to serve top with
1 cup heavy cream, whipped

Meringue Imperial

#1   *10 servings*

A *beautiful creation.*
Beat until stiff

6 egg whites   ⅛ teaspoon salt

Add, 2 tablespoons at a time
2 cups sugar
beating well after each addition.
Add

1 teaspoon vinegar   **½ teaspoon vanilla**

Line a baking sheet with waxed paper and trace on it two circles 9 inches in diameter. Spread circles with meringue. Bake at 275° F for 45 minutes. Reduce heat to 250° F and bake for 15 minutes. Remove to rack. Cool. Freeze if desired or store in covered container. The morning of the day of serving cover surface of 1 meringue with

1 cup heavy cream,   **⅜ cup broken pecan meats**
  whipped   **1 square semisweet choco-**
1½ cups seedless grapes   **late, curled with potato**
1 cup black grapes, seeded   **peeler**

Top with second ring of meringue. Repeat the cover with same amounts of each ingredient. Tuck in here and there
28 pecan halves
Refrigerate until serving time.

Mocha Mousse with Praline Sauce

*#2   *8 servings*
Soften
1 envelope gelatin
in
¼ cup cold strong coffee
Heat together until chocolate melts
¾ cup strong coffee   **1 square unsweetened**
                                   chocolate
Combine with gelatin. Chill until mixture begins to thicken (about 20 minutes). Whip slightly
1 pint heavy cream
Add
Pinch of salt   **1 teaspoon vanilla**
⅔ cup superfine sugar

Fold into mocha mixture. Spoon into 1½ quart mold. Freeze or refrigerate. When ready to serve, defrost and unmold. Serve with Praline Sauce.

PRALINE SAUCE

Heat together in saucepan

2 tablespoons instant coffee powder
¼ cup hot water
1 cup dark corn syrup

⅛ teaspoon salt
¼ cup miniature marshmallows

Simmer 5 minutes. Stir in

½ teaspoon vanilla   1 cup pecans

Refrigerate until ready to serve.

Mousse au Chocolat

#2   *6–8 servings*

Melts in your mouth!
In top of double boiler over hot water melt

½ lb sweet chocolate   ¼ cup sugar
3 tablespoons water

Mix well, remove and cool. Add, one at a time

4 egg yolks

mixing well after each addition. Add

1 inch scraped vanilla bean
Fold in

4 stiffly beaten egg whites

Spoon into individual pots. Refrigerate. To serve, top with

1 cup heavy cream, whipped

Sherry-Almond Soufflé

#2   *12–15 servings*

In saucepan stir until smooth

½ cup sugar
1 cup water
1 cup sweet sherry
1 tablespoon lemon juice

1 envelope plus 2 teaspoons gelatin
7 egg yolks

Cook over medium heat, stirring until mixture coats spoon. Transfer to large bowl. Refrigerate until it reaches consistency of unbeaten egg whites. Line soufflé dish with

1 two and three-fourths-oz package lady fingers

Make collar for 2-quart soufflé dish by folding a 30-inch strip of buttered waxed paper in half lengthwise. Place it butter side in around soufflé dish so that collar stands 3 inches above rim.

Add

¾ cup slivered blanched almonds

to cooked gelatin. Whip

3 cups heavy cream

Beat until they form soft peaks

7 egg whites　　　　　　　　　**¼ teaspoon salt**

Add gradually

¼ cup sugar

Beat until stiff. Fold cream and whites into gelatin. Turn into soufflé dish. Refrigerate at least overnight. To serve top with

1 cup heavy cream, whipped　　**Crystallized violets, if desired**

Tortoni

*　　　　　　　　　　　　　　　　　　　*6–8 servings*

Grind in electric blender enough to make ½ cup plus 2 tablespoons

Hard macaroons

Beat

1 cup heavy cream

Fold in

½ cup macaroon crumbs　　　　**1 egg white, stiffly beaten**
⅓ cup confectioners' sugar, sifted　　**1 tablespoon dry sherry**

Pour mixture into

2-inch paper baking cups

Sprinkle with remaining crumbs. Freeze firm.

Index

Index